BUILT FOR SPEED

JOHN McGUINNESS
BUILT FOR SPEED

MY AUTOBIOGRAPHY
with John Hogan

EBURY
PRESS

9 10 8

Ebury Press, an imprint of Ebury Publishing
20 Vauxhall Bridge Road
London SW1V 2SA

Ebury Press is part of the Penguin Random House group
of companies whose addresses can be found at global.
penguinrandomhouse.com

Copyright © John McGuinness 2017

John McGuinness has asserted his right to be identified as the
author of this Work in accordance with the Copyright, Designs
and Patents Act 1988

First published by Ebury Press in 2017

www.penguin.co.uk

A CIP catalogue record for this book is available from the British
Library

ISBN 9781785034800

Typeset in India by Integra Software Services Pvt. Ltd, Pondicherry

Printed and bound in Great Britain by Clays Ltd, St Ives PLC

 Penguin Random House is committed to a
sustainable future for our business, our readers
and our planet. This book is made from Forest
Stewardship Council® certified paper.

*To my family – my amazing wife Becky, our two kids
Ewan and Maisie, my parents, Becky's mum and dad,
and my wonderful Nana*

CONTENTS

Foreword by Guy Martin

It's early March and me, John and the Honda team are out testing the new Fireblade in the sun. It's going ok; there's a few niggles to sort, but I got to tinker on the bikes and John even trusted me enough to take a spanner to his so I think that is a good sign of things to come. At this point, John asks a favour: would I write a foreword for his new book? John is the man so I say, aye, as long as I can have a bit of input from the boss, and that is Nigel the Dog. John looked at me like my potato bravas were a bit too spicy last night but just says, yeah whatever. John hasn't really met Nigel yet, he will see. I give Nige a call and the conversation goes a bit like this...

Guy: Now Boy, what's happening? Nowt much to report here. The Fireblade is going well and the team are mega. John has asked a favour, though. Can we write a foreword for his book?

(There's a deep sigh on the other end of the phone...)

Nige: Oh dear...

Guy: What's up?

Nige: You do know that people ask their celebrity friends to write forewords? Which means McPint has put you in the celebrity category with his F1 mate and that one from the *Bake Off*.

Guy: What? John knocks about with the old bird?

Nige: Yeah Dad, a bit of enduro in the morning together and supposedly Mary has taught him how to make a mean Victoria sponge.

Guy: Right interesting weekend then.

Nige: Yeah Dad... What do I think of John? John McGuinness will be remembered as an all-time TT legend when he finally retires. The man has 23 wins under his belt and is chasing down Joey's 26-win record, so I don't see him retiring anytime soon. Do I think he can do it? Never underestimate John. I don't know if anyone knows the course as well as him. Sometimes at the beginning of the week you think, ah, he has lost it as he's got no wins, and then he finally arrives at the senior and you can't beat him for love nor money.

Guy: We like John, he seems really happy in his lot, maybe I envy that a bit. He is happy with not chasing something bigger and better every week. He loves the TT: that's his drug of choice. He chases the wins.

Nige: He isn't the fittest of lads. But you can't really argue that beer and pies should be taken off the pre-TT training diet plan, as the results speak for themselves. Perhaps we need to get the pies in you?

Guy: Maybe I can get his mate Mary to give us a recipe then?

Nige: (*sighs*)

We both wish John all the best with the book, it's a great read and John is as down to earth as they come, even when he rocks up in his superstar motorhome. He is quick witted and I like the banter. I am looking forward to being his team mate and I hope you all enjoy the read. Nige? Anything to add?

Nige: Hang about, what this rubbish about being 'just a brickie from Morecambe'? More chances of you laying an egg than a brick, mate.

Guy and Nige

Becky McGuinness on John McGuinness

I'VE HELD JOHN McGuinness's hand and his spare visors for more than 350 races over the last 27 years. From his first race at Aintree in September 1990 until the last time you saw him flagged away down the Glencrutchery road, I've lived and breathed every corner of every single race. The British Championships, World Championships, North Wests, Ulster GPs, TTs, Macaus, Stars of Darleys, Scarboroughs, Daytonas and more. I've done all the worrying, as well as all the washing. It's what any good wife would do for any good husband. Some women don't make very good racer wives and some racers make for terrible husbands. That little bit of glamour that you might see on the telly takes hard work from both sides. The silence while we wait to hear he's through this or that sector of the TT is even more complete when you're the closest person to him. The crashes, the wins, the deaths and all the miles in between, I've laughed and cried with John all the way. I'm the person that sees the

John McGuinness that John doesn't want anyone else to see. Sometimes John doesn't even want to see that John himself. I've seen every side of him whether I've wanted to or not.

I've been with John since I was 13 and I'm now 41. I've supported him through thick and thin, for richer and definitely for poorer. He went wild for a few years and it was a real challenge keeping up with him. Good men like David Jefferies provided a calming influence and helped keep him on, or at least near the right track.

John's biggest problem is that he has the mental age of a 12-year-old. If you think I'm joking, you should have seen him on a recent family day out to York. He spotted a doughnut stand and decided there and then that he needed one of his own. All day he was talking about getting one, trying to convince our 15-year-old son Ewan and anyone else who'd listen. I can understand my son thinking it might be a good idea, but when your 44-year-old husband looks you dead in the eyes and tells you that we need a 'McDoughnut stand' so that he can earn a living on the side from racing, it's as hard to accept as it is ridiculous. I've been watching these kinds of episodes unfold for the last 27 years and they've never got any better. If anything, they've got worse. He does make me laugh though, which is just as well because if I didn't laugh I'd go nuts. Shared laughter is one of the major reasons we're still together. Life is very serious and too much horrible stuff goes on, so it's essential. That said, I would have served less time for murder. In fact, I could have actually murdered him, been released and still had a life in the time that we've been together.

Living with John is easy. All that is required is loving him, racing and motorbikes so much that you'd be willing to live in a freezing-cold tin van on the beach in Morecambe in winter. When we had to do that it was just another adventure, another twist and turn in our journey. Those low points had to happen for us to be able to experience the high points, like when we lived in St Tropez in the same tin van. Lying on the beach and taking water taxis around the bay, or jumping on the scooter with our son when he was a baby were rewards for putting up with the cold a few months before. You could say we were irresponsible but I think most people are when they're young. Also, John's perception of danger on or off a bike is different from nigh on every other person's on the planet. If he feels safe, he's going to do something and maybe part of that has rubbed off on me and how we live. We live with risk day in and day out.

I don't think there's a downside to living with John, aside from the odd tantrum. When he gets on a bike he's a god. Bikers all over the world worship him, wherever we are. But to me, he's my little drama queen. To be fair, in all those races over all those years, the only place

I've ever really seen him stressed is at the TT. By the Tuesday of race week in 2016 he wanted to go home; he was absolutely, completely and utterly deflated. His workload was massive, the bike wasn't as competitive as he'd hoped and things were spiralling out of control. Only John can control that. I can be there to help him but he has to deal with certain situations on his own. He did. He always does.

People have told me over the years that I need to persuade him to give up racing. How can I do that? Who am I to tell him that he has to give up what he enjoys doing most in the world? Nobody has the right to do that to him, not his wife or his family or anyone else. That's my opinion on his racing and maybe that's why we work together. I don't control John, I just do his washing, make sure the holes in his jeans aren't too big and point him at the shower now and then. He's worked harder than most people will ever understand to live the life you're about to read about. I hope you enjoy reading it as much as we've enjoyed living it.

Becky McGuinness
December 2016

CHAPTER 1

Moon Head Baby

I WAS BORN on 16 April 1972 at the Queen Victoria hospital in Morecambe. I was delivered using forceps and weighed 8lbs 6oz, most of which was made up by my huge head. I was basically pulled out of my mother by an enormous set of mole grips. Apparently, back in the early seventies the normal thing to do was to put you in an incubator when you first arrived. When they carried me back to my mum after I'd been cleaned up and sorted out, she took one look at me and said, 'What's that?'

I had a massive head which, even after half an hour in the incubator, was still covered in marks from the mole grips. They told her I clearly hadn't wanted to come out yet and that it had taken a fair bit of work to pull me out. Me and my mum still laugh about how shocked she must have been when she realised she'd given birth to a baby with a moon head.

Less than two miles from the hospital was 52 Granville Road, the McGuinness family home at the time. A three-bedroom terraced house, it's two streets back from the

Promenade in Morecambe and less than ten minutes from where you catch the ferry to the Isle of Man.

My dad, John McGuinness senior, was working on the tools in a bike shop in Morecambe when I was born. My mum Christine has always worked; she's a Trojan, a proper grafter. She worked at a place called Cannon Hygiene, managing toilet rubbish facilities and chemicals. I can't remember too much about the early days, but from what I've been told I spent a lot of time getting dropped off at my Nana's house while my mum and dad were out working. The connection I had with my Nana was massive and I suppose it started before I can even remember.

*

Three years after I was born, my brother Andrew came along. We shared a room, had bunk beds and spent a lot of time together, but it was clear from an early age that he was a bit of a nutter. He was the kind of kid who, if we went to the zoo, would have his hand over the fence trying to stroke a tiger. He was just fearless. I found him once, floating face down in Sandylands swimming pool on the beach in Morecambe. He was just a toddler and had clearly climbed in for a little swim, unaware of the dangers. I don't think my mum or anyone else had realised that he was in there. I'd like to be able to say I leapt in and pulled him out like a hero, but in fact I just pointed and shouted, 'Look, Mum. Andrew's swimming!' My mum leapt in without a thought and pulled him out in a flash. Who knows how close to drowning he was. He would climb anything, set fire to everything and generally cause carnage wherever he went. If he wasn't sticking pencils up our Alsatian's nose, he was trying to ride the thing round the house.

We had a decorator round once who was a bit nervous of Sam. He kept asking if the dog was going to bite him and jumped any time the it walked near him. Eventually he got to work up a ladder, scraping a wall or whatever. When I heard the guy screaming in agony, I guessed the dog had finally bitten him and went running in to see what was going on. He was screaming at us to get the dog off him, but when I ran into the room, it was my baby brother who had his teeth buried in the painters' arse. We had to peel him off.

Andrew was a loving kid though. As soon as he could speak he would tell me that he loved me. He still does now when I see him. I'm a bit weird when it comes to expressing myself to anyone apart from my wife and kids, but Andrew's never had a problem with it. I know without a doubt that he'd fight to the death to defend me. He's never lost the fiery side he had as a kid. Take his first day at Sandylands primary school for example. It's a fairly big deal for most kids. It was for our Andrew too, at least for the hour that he lasted before he was sent home for trashing the classroom. The teacher who sent him home was called Mrs Benstead and I think she was too weak to deal with him. He needed keeping in check and he needed someone with some patience to help bring him on. She didn't have it in her to stick with him and gave up before she'd even given him a chance. I often wonder if that first day at school was the trigger that set him off on a path that he's never really been able to get off. He's had his problems to deal with over the years, fought with his own demons and I wish I could turn the clock back for him.

*

It's hard to work out if my earliest memory is genuine or just an image lodged in my brain from looking at pictures of myself when I was a kid. Either way, there's a motorbike in there, obviously. Real memory or not, I brimmed the fuel tank on my Italjet 50 with water when I was three years old. I thought it would run on it when I'd used all the petrol that was in the tiny tank. My dad went mental at me and turned it upside down like you would with a BMX when you have to put the chain back on. He had to drain all the water out of it and he gave me a bollocking while he sorted it out.

We had no child-minder or anything so when my dad went to work at his garage, if I wasn't at my Nana's house I'd go with him and just hang around. While he was spannering bikes or talking to customers, I'd be sticking my hands in exhausts or pulling tools off the bench. My dad would be in and out of the workshop, or out on the forecourt doing a deal on some old car, and customers would be in and out all day. If it was cold, he'd build a fire in a 45-gallon drum for us to keep warm around. When I got bored of listening to dad and his pals talking about bikes, I'd toddle off for a ride round the estate on my bike. At first it had stabilisers but they were quickly removed. Once I'd figured out how to make the little bike stop and start around the yard, I was off. I used to ride it round our streets for what felt like hours. The police stopped me on it once and took me home for riding it on the road without a helmet. I was about four years old.

When I'd grown up, I used to meet people in the pub who had bought bikes and cars from big John McGuinness and could remember me as a toddler in the workshop, or they'd seen me flying round the place on that little Italjet. If a kid rides a bike like that round a housing estate now, a police helicopter chases them and their bike ends up getting crushed. Back then, nobody was really bothered. I'd buzz past people and it was just little John, having a ride on his motorbike, scrambling round in the gravel or building jumps and ramps out of whatever he could get his little hands on.

In those early days, I had nobody to ride with and just used to race myself. My dad would watch when he had a minute, or I'd go and pester him to look at me do a bit of a wheelie or a skid. He'd always find the time. He was my hero and I looked up to him. You always look up to your dad no matter how old you get, don't you? Even if I didn't like him at times I always respected him. There were some brutal dads around Morecambe at that time. Most of them seemed to be piss heads who just wanted to fight all the time. Things were definitely different back then. My dad liked a pint and wasn't scared of scrapping with anyone, but he didn't let that side of him take over his life like some of the other guys at the time.

I can't remember if I outgrew the little Italjet or if someone offered my dad a good deal for it. Knowing his character, if somebody had dangled a bit of profit in front of him, it would have been sold before you knew it. Anyway, off it went and it was replaced with a Malaguti 50, which was a slightly bigger bike. Motorbikes were just kind of there for whenever I wanted to get on one or kick one around the workshop.

*

Eventually the Malaguti was replaced with a Suzuki RM50. By this time, I'd outgrown riding round the yard and the local fields, and my dad was keen to see how I'd get on in a race. I was only six or seven years old and, I won't lie, I was shitting my pants at the prospect. We loaded everything up into the van for the drive to the track, which was short as it was a local race. By the time we got there I was screaming about how I didn't want to ride. My dad kept saying that I'd be fine once I got going and to just get on with it. Pre-race nerves are completely natural, I know that now. But back then I had no idea what was going on, and as I was putting my kit on I felt like a condemned man. It was horrible. I'd bottled it before we'd even lined up to race. It felt like one minute I was riding round the yard at my dad's workshop with a smile on my face and the next I was being thrown to the lions. My head was pounding, I felt sick one minute and wanted to lie down the next. At the last second before the race started, I burst into tears and pleaded with my dad to take me home. Dad went mental, screaming at me to get in the back of the van with the bike. He wouldn't let me sit in the front with him and drove off like a loony, kit and bikes and me flying all over the place in the back. Eventually he calmed down and took me to a quiet practice track and gave me a run out before we went home.

He was the worst schoolboy motocross dad in the world. From that first miserable attempt at racing on the RM50 all the way through to when I packed in schoolboy racing as a teenager and traded my MX bike for a Yamaha TZR125, my dad would think nothing of letting me know what he thought about my performance. He sometimes left me stranded at MX meetings, having decided I was shit while I was out on the bike, packed the van up and driven home leaving me and the bike behind. I'd have to get a lift back with my mates. When I got home hours later he'd have calmed down enough to explain what it was that I was doing wrong.

I enjoyed making friends and the camaraderie of going racing. Even when young lads aren't winning races they're learning about paddock life and everything that brings. At schoolboy level you'd probably get a trophy for coming tenth, so there was always a pot to bring home. Sometimes I'd have a good ride and other times I'd be very average. This infuriated my dad because it was hard for him to figure out why I'd been quicker or slower that day. I'd normally just be happy to carry my plastic trophy for finishing eighth through the paddock and would proudly prop it up on the dashboard of the van for the drive home. Sometimes I'd be driving home with my head down, staring at my feet while dad bollocked me for not getting a result and other days I'd have my feet on the dash and a smile the size of a dustbin lid, jabbering away about the race and how much fun I'd had out there.

I think the same thing about MX now as I did back then and that is that it's a tough old game. I think it would be harder to be a world class MX racer than it would to be a world class road racer. I don't mean any disrespect to anybody but that's how I feel. The training required is constant and the risk of injury seems much higher. The top guys always seem to hampered by niggly injuries. Being good at MX doesn't seem too hard, but being great at it is a massive challenge, one that I just don't think I was ready to face when I was a schoolboy. Even when you don't fall off it hurts. I was forever coming home with skin hanging off and bruises everywhere. I broke my knee pretty badly one time and I just hated crashing, which happens a lot in the sport. What was the point? I never really had any success worth writing home about. I won a few scrambles here and there and that was it. I raced in AMCA, a class that was slightly easier than the ACU MX series, I reckon. I progressed through junior to senior class, won a few races and then moved up to expert level, but was only ever a mid-pack racer at that stage.

There were longs periods between MX races when it feels like I just wasn't that interested in racing. It's a period of my life that I've forgotten a lot about, which tells me that I can't have been enjoying it too much when I was doing it. When something pulls that trigger of interest in my head, I get to know a subject inside out and can recall the tiniest details, but if something doesn't grab my attention, I quickly forget about it and move onto the next thing. That's how I look back at the MX days and my time at school. I also don't think I allowed myself to get too attached to the bikes or the racing in case they dried up. There was no structure to the way we went racing so I just used to do it for a bit of fun. Plus, as I said, one minute I had a bike and the next my dad had converted it into cash to put into a car deal or something.

*

It's hard to pin down the poster bike that I wanted back then. When I was really young it was all about MX bikes. They were the ones I was cutting out of magazines like *Motorcycle Weekly* and *MCN* and sticking to my wall. It's weird, because it's not as if I massively enjoyed riding motocross. But I liked the bikes and liked having pictures of them on the walls. By the time I was twelve or thirteen, I had a bit of a thing for Suzuki RG500s. I'm guessing it was down to Barry Sheene and the fact that my dad raced one as well. I think it was the four exhaust pipes. Standing next to one and seeing the smoke coming out of them just did it for me. There's still something about that bike that grabs me every time I see one.

My first encounter with a big fast bike must have been riding on the back of something that my dad was servicing in the shop. He'd need to test ride them when he'd finished working on them and when I was big enough to jump on the back we'd be off. I know we went on Kawasaki Z900s and Z1300s. Big fast beasts like them and Norton Commandos were always fun to get rides on. Weirdly, though, it was a little Suzuki X7 that Dad scared the life out of me on one time. For those who don't know, an X7 is a 250cc two-stroke that made less than 30 horsepower. They had no right to be as fast and as scary as they were, but for whatever reason they just flew. My dad wasn't shy when it came to speed. Car or bike, he'd soon have the thing flat out, no seatbelt on and not a care in the world, sailing off humpback bridges, doing jumps and pissing about. It was always a thrill to do stuff with my dad, whether it was eating in a café and legging it without paying or him getting into a scrap somewhere. Never a dull moment.

CHAPTER 2

Crackling Radio

NOTHING ASSAULTS YOUR senses like a bike coming flat out down Bray Hill. First there's the anticipation, hearing the commentator talking the rider towards you on the radio. Then you pick up the roar in the distance. Even now, even for me, that first time they come down the hill is a shock. Your reaction when first you feel the breath being sucked out of your body as a bike rips through the air what feels like inches from your face will stay with you forever. It looks impossible. It shouldn't be happening so close to you.

The first time I went to the Isle of Man was in 1982, when I was about ten. I already knew about the place because I'd heard people talking about it in my dad's garage. The place was obviously always full of bikers and the TT would regularly pop up in conversation. I'm sure it was the same in bike shops up and down the country, but the fact we were only minutes from Heysham ferry port, which is where you get the boat to the Isle of Man, made it feel like our local race. My mum and dad had been going together for years and I'd read about it in magazines. I knew it was only a matter of time before I got to go there.

There was no Internet or social media then so I had to read bike magazines and MCN every week to see what everyone was up to. I'd hoover all that up and then sit and listen to my dad and his mates telling stories about riding flat out on the roads on the Isle of Man. Then, suddenly, I was there myself, just another face in the crowd watching the bikes fly by. Finally, I got to experience the smells, the noise and the speed for real. The radio crackling away next to me just added to the atmosphere. It was like a massive injection in my head and it blew my fucking mind. I knew within seconds of seeing the bikes go by for the first time that I was going to be a TT racer. I didn't know how and I knew my dad wasn't going to be keen. Everyone around me knew the dangers. But from that moment I knew I had to do it.

When I first saw the TT with my own eyes, I was sitting on a grass bank with my feet hanging over the edge at Bray Hill. Joey Dunlop went through, then Crosby, then Haslam, Alex George, Stu Avant, all these super heroes, seemingly just inches away from me.

People might not agree, but I think I needed to grow up on a race bike somewhere else before I tried it. I still think that now. You've got to be a man to race that place. I didn't race at the TT until 1996 when I was 24 years old. Some of the boys now are too young, way too fucking young. There's too much pressure on them. Look at poor Wayne Hamilton, 20 years old when he was killed at the 13th milestone in the Manx in 2011. By the time I lined up to race there, I'd done thousands of miles on race bikes. I'd hit my head on the floor a few times, I'd lost money racing and I'd won money racing. I'd had sponsors, I understood engines and tyres and what was what before I went there. On the flip side, Michael Dunlop went there at 18 and he's arguably one of the best road racers ever. But I still think you're vulnerable as a road racer when you're young.

Anyway, at ten years old, I knew I was going to be a TT rider one day. I was definitely having some of that! My dad did a bit of road racing at Jurby on the roads up at the north end of the Isle of Man, and I'd sit on the grass, all pumped up, watching him race. These races took place during practice week for the TT, which meant we'd be there for four or five days. He'd regularly finish in the top six. I used to feel so proud. Seeing him bring the first 350 home against the newer and quicker RG Suzukis made us both feel great. He was a good rider.

When he said we were setting off for home at the end of that first week I went mental, screaming that I wanted to stay and watch more bikes on the TT course. He shouted at me to help him get things packed up. On the way home, I stood on the ferry crying as the Isle of Man disappeared behind us. I didn't want to let the place out of my sight. It was like I'd found my perfect playground.

We repeated that pattern for a few years, never being able to fit in the full TT fortnight because of school for me and work for my dad.

*

Dad's bike shop was called McGuinness' motorcycles. He did MOTs and servicing at a time when bikes were selling really well. There was always a deal going on. I often wonder what would have happened if my dad had made a few better business decisions. When I look at Padgett's or Fowlers motorcycles now, I think things could have been very different.

The early 1970s was the right time to be in the bike industry but my dad was too busy enjoying life to go all-in. He'll probably hate me for saying that, but it's true. He liked a drink and he liked a scrap and he loved his MX. He didn't focus on making the business as big as it could have been. I also reckon he was given some bad advice along the way. It grieves me now to think about the missed opportunity. There are a lot of those early dealerships still around. They got things right back then to the point where if bike sales aren't so good they can still do all right as businesses, renting out yards or buildings that they've picked up along the way.

Things are completely different now. Opening a dealership today just looks so hard. My dad won't take me thinking he made a few mistakes on the chin. But this is a man who was due to race in the 1984 Manx Grand Prix and missed the ferry to the Isle of Man. And we lived in Heysham, where the bloody boat leaves from! People from Austria, Switzerland, Germany and France – all over the world, in fact – manage to get to Heysham to catch the ferry. We lived round the corner and we missed it. Obviously, Dad blamed his mate, who was doing some car deal. But I wouldn't have waited for anything. I'd have been on that boat and gone. Maybe that's just me. I love my dad to bits. I respect him and it's clear that without him I wouldn't be where I am today. At the same time, I do believe that these things sometimes happen for a reason. He was a good racer though.

*

I went to the TT in 1986 with my dad on the back of a Honda CB900. I was 14 and riding a 125 MX bike at the time and I thought I was quick, but when I got on the back of that thing round the island, it scared the shit out of me. Dad knew his way around and would get a shift on.

That year I met Joey Dunlop. He was with Rothmans Honda on a factory RVF in a garage at the bottom of the TT paddock. At the time the 500cc Grand Prix two strokes were also painted in Rothmans colours, so Joey's RVF looked fucking trick. Plus his Kushitani made-to-measure leathers with the yellow lid looked perfect. He just looked the bollocks, hair dangling out the back as he went by. I'd hang around in the paddock and wait to see him cutting around. I decided I wanted his autograph and bought a picture of him from a shop, went back up to the paddock and started asking people where I could find him so he could sign it. He never said much and was usually a bit grumpy about something. On that day in 1986, while he was silently signing his autograph on the picture I'd handed him, I looked up at him and told him that I'd be up on the podium with him one day. He looked down and mumbled something that I couldn't understand. It was only a dream at the time but it felt completely natural to say that to him.

The first time I saw Joey riding at the TT was in 1982 during that first visit when I was ten. Rocket Ron Haslam actually won the race – Joey came second ahead of Dave Hiscock – but there was just something about Joey. It wasn't like the first time I saw him he immediately became my hero. There were other fast guys that I followed, men who raced full factory bikes and also deserved to be heroes. I'd followed them all, hoovering up every line of every race report I could put my hands on, so to see any of them in real life felt like a real privilege. But Joey quickly became my number one.

I can remember one time in particular that seemed to cement Joey's hero status for me. I was on the island on my BMX, pedalling about in a world of my own. I could hear a race bike coming but the roads were open to the public and there were cars driving up and down. I wasn't sure what was going on so I stopped and looked up the road. It was Joey. He was on a full factory RVF750 with his long hair and his cool yellow helmet, wearing a Rothmans paddock jacket and a pair of jeans. He wasn't trying to look cool, he was just Joey, doing what he did, but I thought he was cool as fuck. He'd just popped out of the paddock for a packet of fags. My jaw hit the floor as I saw him pull up and lean his race bike against the window of the paper shop up from Villa Marina. I can still hear the bike ticking over in my head like it was yesterday, with its big long exhaust burbling away. I was just a snotty-nosed kid and he didn't even know I was there. He came out and brapped his way back towards the paddock. I was absolutely in awe and Joey instantly became a god to me. It is something I'll never forget.

Joey, God rest him, rode some beautiful bikes. In the early 80's, those Honda RS850s were superior to anything else. Joey Dunlop and Honda looked like a winning combination to me. When you're a kid you're drawn to success. Joey was breaking lap records and racking up races and I wanted to follow him because he was a winning machine. Everybody does that. Winners inspire people, I see that from the other side of the fence now. People walk past the guy who finished fourth at the TT to meet the guy that came first.

I understand now why I was as drawn to Joey Dunlop as I was. That is the nature of racing success. To me, he was the absolute bollocks. I couldn't wait to get hold of *Motorcycle News* when my dad was finished with it so I could keep up with what he was doing and cut his pictures out for my scrap book or to go on my bedroom wall. After 1989, Joey didn't win a race at the TT for about 20 years, until we were teammates on the VTRs.

*

In 1987 and 1988 I went to the TT on my own, first on my BMX and then on a Peugeot racing bike. I used to grab onto a van as it drove onto the side-loading boat from Heysham to Douglas, getting a free tow. The drivers would present their tickets, window down, chatting to the man in the booth and I'd be hiding on the opposite side. Nobody would see me get on and nobody would notice me sitting on the boat on my own. I used to get on the boat that left at two in the morning. I'd be there in time for practice in the morning then sneak back on a boat and be home the same day.

I was on Bray Hill when Steve Hislop won his first TT in 1987. He was leading the Junior race on his Formula

2 bike by a mile, until his ignition went and he broke down. Then he won the Formula 2 race. Being there was brilliant. I was just a kid, sat with my feet dangling off a wall, BMX in a bush behind me, loving every second of it.

When I swapped my BMX for a Peugeot racing bike, I used the same tactic to sneak on the boat. This time, though, I took a tent and a few bits and pieces so that I could stay for a few days. I'd have been about 16. At that age, I can't think of a single place I'd have rather been than in my little tent on the Isle of Man.

CHAPTER 3

Pedalling Towards the Boat

SCHOOL WAS A weird time for me. I wasn't a bad kid, just a bit yappy. More of a pain in the arse than a problem child. I've still got my old reports from Heysham High School. One that stands out says this: 'John is not applying himself at school. He is too happy to talk about anything other than work. He is not without ability, but is wasting his own time.' 'Noisy' and 'entertaining' are words that crop up on some of my classroom reports, but you'll also find 'lazy', 'inattentive' and 'motorbikes'.

Whether I was popular or not didn't really matter to me. I was the scruffiest bastard in the world. I never had a haircut or trendy clothes. I was spending a fair amount of time at home looking after my little brother and it made more sense to make sure we'd been fed than to care about the shape of my hair or whether I had the same trainers as everyone else. That lack of drive to be popular meant that I didn't have a huge circle of mates, so I don't have many friends from my time at school any

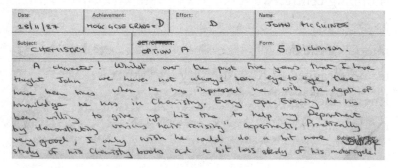

Bunsen burners, chemicals, heat and a bit of danger – exactly what most schoolboys were into. I definitely was.

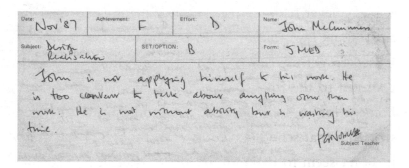

Yes another teacher telling me I was wasting my time thinking about motorbikes. I wonder what that teacher is up to now…

more. I stay in touch with one or two but I've never been to a school reunion or anything like that.

I remember nicking off school once with a mate called Jason Morgan and a few others. We went to the Arndale shopping centre. We thought we were invincible as well as invisible, despite being in our school uniforms in the middle of the day in a shopping centre. The police caught us and dragged us back to school and that was it for me, I never did anything like that again. I really didn't like the feeling of being in deep shit. I always seemed to be in trouble for minor things and spent most of my school time on some kind of report, but this was different. I'm not sure if it was the fact the police caught us, but I didn't bother nicking off again.

I was never really into fighting or being nasty at that age. I think I was just a cheeky pain in the arse. At home I used to get away with a lot but at school I had to conform to the rules. I was left to my own devices at home a lot so, looking back, maybe I appreciated the structure that school gave me, even though at the time it didn't seem to make much sense. I seemed to spend most of my time drawing cocks and articulated trucks on books. In fact, I'm surprised to this day that I can read or write.

I did feel that some of my teachers hated me because they just didn't get the fact that I wanted to be a professional bike racer. One day we had to stand up to do a talk on a subject of our choice. Obviously I chose motorbikes and racing. Other kids took the chance to show off their favourite football strip. I wheeled my RM125 into the classroom and spoke about what it felt like to race it.

I did get on with my chemistry teacher, Mr Rose. He was a right strict bastard though. We had a love-hate relationship but we saw eye-to-eye on most subjects. There was something about him that I respected. He was a chubby Jock who was happy for us to have a laugh, but could maintain discipline when he needed to. I liked that. My school report from him says, 'John is always willing to give up his time to help with open evenings, by demonstrating various hair -raising experiments. Practically very good. I only wish he could do a bit more study of his chemistry books and a bit less study of his motorcycle'. When you're young and there's Bunsen burners on the go everywhere and magnesium to burn, you're never going to be too interested in learning about the periodic table, are you? I know I wasn't. I just wanted to burn stuff.

Becky ended up having Mr Rose as a form tutor a few years later, when I'd left school. He saw that she had written 'Becky loves John McGuinness' on one of her books and told her she could do far better than dating me. Twenty-seven years later me and Becky are still going strong.

I'll be honest, I don't have answers for some of my school reports. 'John is proceeding sluggishly with his coursework and is going to have very little choice about what he can show in his exhibition because of the low volume of his work. He has still to hand in his museum project which is now one year overdue.' That was from Art and Design, which I remember being one of my better classes. I can't really explain where that year went, it's still lost in my head. Why would they let me get away with handing things in a year overdue? Maybe the teacher had given up on me. I'm aware that my organisation skills are average at best. But If I say something is going to get done, then it'll get done. It might end up being at the 12th hour, but it'll happen.

I didn't not care about school exactly, but it didn't mean that much to me. I missed some chemistry and English tests in 1988 because I was on the Isle of Man watching the races. I can remember being on my pushbike and having to make the choice of riding to school or the ferry to go and watch the TT. My legs were pedalling towards the boat before I'd even made my mind up. That says it all really. That's not because I was a bad person and wanted to rebel, there was just something about the island that just drew me to it every single time.

*

Lots of people who know me now say that my attention span is tiny. If I'm not into what's going on around me, my mind wanders and I start to find things to do that do grab my attention. I think this has applied throughout my life. I saw road racing on the Isle of Man at such an early stage that I probably compare pretty much everything I look at to it. If it's not interesting enough, then I switch off.

Apparently, now I have the brain of a 25-year-old. Every year, Dunlop Tyres send me off to a weird medical facility where they carry out tests on my brain to see how I deal with situations that would shock the average adult. It involves sitting at a screen that shows a sequence of random numbers. I have to look for patterns and touch the screen when I see one. In between the numbers, they expose you to horrendous images. Graphic scenes of violence, injured and disfigured people and other horrible stuff. Last year, I did the tests back-to-back against some journalists, who couldn't blinker the negative stimuli. For some reason, I can blank out the shocking images. Even when something has my attention, I seem to be better at dealing with it if I leave it to the last minute. Bills that need to be paid, jobs that desperately need doing, whatever it is will get done, but only when it suits me or when there is no option.

*

When I was 15, my mum bought me a Suzuki AP50. It had straight bars and I made a homemade seat unit for it that weighed about eight tons. It looked ridiculous but I was into tinkering and wanted to get it ready to ride for the day I turned 16. I used to keep it in my Nana's shed until one day someone burnt the whole lot down while it was in there. I was devastated. I never really got to the bottom of how it happened, but the outside toilet and the coal shed were burned to the ground as well. I was so upset that everyone clubbed together and bought me another one for my 16th birthday. I remember coming downstairs on the big day and finding the replacement bike waiting for me in the hallway. I had no idea that was going to happen and was blown away that people around me cared so much.

Those days on that little bike were ace! Having a road bike meant freedom. What a feeling when you're 16 years old and you get a licence! It doesn't matter if you can only do 30mph, or if the wind is coming at you at 45 degrees, you just don't give a shit. I used to be so pumped to go anywhere on it and would ride it to school, the shops and anywhere else I could think of. Christ knows how many miles I did on it. I fell off that AP loads of times though and wiped the front off too many times to remember.

I remember unscrewing the badge off the tank and smoothing it over with filler, before hand-painting it red and white. It looked rubbish, but when you're 16 you don't give a shit about that do you? I gave it a Micron exhaust and a K&N filter, getting a hand file inside the ports and blowing the bloody thing up every other week. My dad was always on hand to help get it sorted out.

One time I lost the front on the way into a place called Middleton. Water used to run across the road there and down I went. I refused to let go of the handlebars and it dragged me down the road, scraping everything as it went. I kept the clutch in and the engine carried on running. I picked it and myself up and just wobbled off, wondering what the fuck had just happened. I was just flat out on the thing everywhere, there isn't really any other way to ride those little bikes.

One of my mates had an SS50, the other had a Fizzy. We'd bomb about together trying to pull wheelies to impress anyone who might be looking. One day I fell off the AP at a place called Cuerden Park and broke my knee, I had to have a full cast from my balls to my ankles. I really struggled to get round right-handers with that cast on! If I got it wrong, the leg would hit the floor and pick me up off the bike.

I did enjoy some bits of school. Lessons that involved using my hands would always get my attention. Making stuff out of metal was probably my favourite activity. My mate and me made an exhaust for his SS50 as a school project once. It was mint. I enjoyed it so much that I even stayed after school a couple of times to work on it with him. The day we finished it, we were desperate for the bell to ring so we could go and test this pipe on the bike. We raced through Bolton-le-Sands. I used to treat a section of that road like my own mini-Ballaugh Bridge. You had to come down a couple of gears, brake then turn and straighten up for a jump over a bridge. I'd been over it loads of times before and was leading my mate on the SS50 fitted with the pipe we'd made. It was rubbish, to be honest, and didn't make the bike go any faster. It was worse than the one we'd replaced, in fact – it just made loads of noise. Anyway, I was out front on my AP50, mid-air over mini-Ballaugh Bridge, when a guy in a Montego pulled out of the Packet Boat pub right in front of me. I had no chance: my wheels weren't on the ground so I couldn't even brake. I landed and smashed straight into his door, head-butting him through his open window. My AP50 made a right mess of his car.

After rolling down the road a bit, I started picking myself up. Just as I was gathering my thoughts, I heard my mate dropping down through the gears and lining up for the jump on the other side of the bridge. He flew over it and piled into the bits of the car that I'd managed to miss. By the time we were finished, every panel on one side was done in and the car looked like a banana. I started shouting at the guy, going nuts at him like it was his fault. I think he must have had one too many lunchtime beers, because no one ended up claiming off anyone else. Still, looking back I can see that it wasn't really his fault.

It's not every day you pull out and a couple of airborne 50cc bikes come at you from nowhere. I was desperate for my dad not to find out I'd crashed, so I kicked my AP50 straight and wobbled off, once again scratching my head wondering what had just gone on.

I used to blow that thing up almost weekly. Luckily you could get a new motor for it from the scrapyard for about 40 quid and fit it in about eight minutes, it was a great little bike to work on. I tried everything to get it to go quicker, usually resulting in losing speed. I filed the disc valve by hand and all that bollocks. Nothing seemed to work and it'd have been a better job if I'd left the thing alone but I couldn't help it. I used to convince myself that I was just on the verge of unleashing a load of free speed, so out the file would come again.

CHAPTER 4

Meet the Family

I THINK MY mum and dad splitting up while I was going through high school probably didn't help in terms of my studying. Their marriage was never great in the first place. My parents got together when they were kids; they were only 16. My dad lived a bit of a rock-and-roll lifestyle: drinking, fighting and chasing women. Their marriage was pretty shitty, basically, with lots of arguing, shouting and lying. Eventually it boiled over and they went their separate ways.

When my mum and dad split up, Mum went off the rails. She struggled to cope with the whole thing. She was amazing when Becky and me were young and she'd give me the last quid in her purse in a heartbeat, but she carries a lot of resentment towards my dad and his wife Pam. Thirty years later, she can still tie herself in knots about it all. Those were horrible times. My dad was out of the house, living with Pam, and watching my mum struggle to cope on her own was tough.

My brother Andrew was hard work back then and still has problems. As I mentioned, he was expelled from primary school on that first day. It turns out he was in Becky's class, or at least he was until he threw a chair across the room at the teacher. So things weren't looking too good for him even then. Much like me, he'd never really been told what to do at home, so when somebody tried to do it at school he just flipped out. My mum spent a lot of time working long hours, leaving me at home to look after Andrew on my own. Maybe that's the reason why I always look scruffy now. Clean clothes didn't matter to me much back then and not much has changed. We never had any nice clothes to wear, I was the boy getting the piss taken out of him at school because of how I looked.

Andrew was always a little bastard. He was constantly up to something. Sniffing petrol and looking for ways to get high as a kite. He's got a piece missing somewhere that makes him want to do things like that. Right from the word go he was that way. I can remember seeing him sniffing the petrol on my dad's CZ MX bike when he was a baby. It was like he'd had something injected into him at the outset. I didn't want to be like that. When I was a kid I used to look in bike magazines and MCN and see Grand Prix riders sitting in speedboats and stuff. I used to stare at these pictures wondering how they'd managed it and how I could get to do the same thing. Why are these guys traveling all over the world to race motorbikes, to win TTs at the Isle of Man? They were gods to me and I wanted to be the same. I don't know what my brother was thinking about. He ended up in one of those bad-boy schools. He would board there in the week and would just come home at the weekends. When we took him back he'd go mental. It was a nightmare.

My mum still holds a grudge about the way Andrew's life has gone. She compares his struggle with the opportunities that my stepbrother Kurt has had. Kurt joined the RAF and has always worked. He likes going on the piss a bit but he wants to live the dream, so he knuckles down. Andrew has never been prepared to do that bit. He was given chances to work but he let people down. Drugs and the dole were always more important. He's never once shown us that he can be anything other than hard work. I think he's had a drug habit since he was about nine, hiding gas canisters up his sleeves and getting high whenever he could. That developed into a full-on addiction and he'd do anything to feed it, robbing things and so on. My dad wasn't there to control him because he was working off-shore on the rigs by this stage. Meanwhile, my mum was burying her head in the sand rather than dealing with the problem. When I say that none of what I've got was handed to me, I really mean it.

When my dad found a new partner in Pam I was expected to just get on with things, but I didn't like her when I was young. Your mum is your mum and you respect her. When you suddenly find yourself living with your dad and another lady and you want a biscuit and she says no, you flip your lid. Well, I did anyway. I was thought she was too strict and when she bollocked me I wasn't having any of it. We never really got on, until about 15 years ago. Now we're fine. I think she's the best thing since sliced bread and she's good to my family and kids.

Anyway, when I didn't like the way Pam was telling me what to do, we'd get into argy bargy and I wanted out of the way. So I moved from the west end of Morecambe up to Heysham to live with my Nana. She was ace, a right old stalwart but she was my rock. I was about 14 when I first moved in. She was in her early 70s but she wasn't afraid to bollock me and I loved her to pieces.

Hitler flattened my Nana's house in Hackney during the war. Like many others, she was relocated outside London, and Morecambe became home for her and my granddad. He was an air-raid warden during the war and was from Belfast. I've still got relations over in Ireland through him. When he legged it from Ireland he ended up in Hackney, where he met my Nana. I don't know much about what he got up to when he moved to Hackney. He was a fucking grumpy bastard. A Catholic, originally from the Falls Road area, he'd had it hard.

Nana was a massive part of my life growing up, right from the early days when I used to spend time with her while my mum and dad were out working. She raised me when was a baby, really. I was always her favourite grandson, or I thought so anyway. She was up for anything. I remember blagging to her that the Cyclone (a mental rollercoaster on the seafront in Morecambe) was just a gentle ride, so she jumped on it with me. She screamed the place down but laughed the whole way round.

She used to come on holiday with us when we were kids, all round Europe. Dad would be driving a Vauxhall Cresta or whatever car he'd done a deal on that week. He'd be going at it like a lunatic to Spa or somewhere similar to watch the racing. We'd be in the back with Nana screaming at him to slow down while our luggage flew off the roof and down a bank by the side of the road.

Back then I used to cycle everywhere on my BMX. I used to do a paper round on it and go and work in a butchers after school as well. I earned £3.60 a week for the paper round and £3.80 from the butcher's. Then a fiver on top for a full day's work at the butcher's on a Saturday. My Nana was brilliant. I'd get up for school and she'd have my breakfast ready and waiting for me. I'd cycle home from school at lunchtime and she'd have my lunch ready. I'd go straight to the butcher's after school and when I got home, she'd have my tea on the table as I got through the door. It felt like she lived to look after me and I loved it.

I used to help her out a bit, running to the shop to get bread and bits and pieces for her. She was a bit of a battle-axe and spent her whole life smoking Senior Service fags. She was always wheezing and coughing. If she walked to the end of the road she'd be in tatters. She claimed that she'd given up the fags a few times, but then I'd smell it on her or find the odd dog-end here and there.

Her house was proper old-school, with Rosary beads hanging about the place and pictures of Jesus and Mary everywhere. When we were kids we didn't have a clue what that stuff meant to her and used to take the piss, swinging the beads around, asking her what they were for. There were loads of McGuinnesses so there were always kids about the place. My dad had three brothers so at Christmas all of us kids would end up together, off to St Patrick's church and then on to the Christmas do. Most of that lot are all still practising Catholics, so there were First Communions and all the rest of it. My dad was never particularly religious, so me and Andrew were like, 'Nah, we don't fancy that'.

My granddad was a staunch Catholic. Tommy was proper aggro. I just thought he was a cranky bastard. He worked at ICI on night shifts. Waking him up in the daytime before he'd had enough sleep was the worst thing you could do. It'd start with him banging the life out of the floor, to tell us lot downstairs to keep it down and would end with him charging down the stairs shouting the odds at whoever he could find. But he is the boy, he's the original McGuinness who came along all those years ago and built the family. Nana and Tommy were a Cockney and a Paddy against the world.

Tommy got Alzheimer's in the end, but we were only kids at the time didn't understand, so we used to laugh at him while he walked round talking to himself. We'd ask him if he was okay just so that we could laugh at the way he replied. Whenever we used to see him coming we'd shout, 'Fucking leg it!' and run the other way. It got pretty sad eventually and he ended up in Moor hospital in Lancaster with all the other head-bangers.

CHAPTER 5

Becky

I DIDN'T TAKE much notice of the fact that Becky lived exactly opposite my Nana's house when I first moved in because she was just a squirt. A little squidhead. I used to kick around with a few of the girls. I sort of fancied a girl who live nearby for a bit but she was a fucking loony. I say I fancied her, but you don't really know what's what at that age, apart from how to play with your knob.

I started dating Becky on 28 March 1989. She was hanging out of the bedroom window at her friend's house when I shouted up to her to ask if she'd be my girlfriend. We'd been friends for a while, just talking and that. When we started going out she was 13 and I was 16. I can remember my chat-up line. I asked her if she wanted to come and see my Suzuki RM125 and my plastic MX trophies, which were up at my dad's house in my old bedroom. He lived about a mile away so our first date was the walk up to his place to have a look at my motocross bike. Then I took her upstairs to see my trophies.

I can remember my stepmum growling a bit about it at the time, 'What's going on up them stairs! Get yourselves down here now!' She was probably panicking about the age gap between the two of us. But our first date just involved a motorbike and a look at my trophies. Above them I had the word 'JOEY' spelled out on the wall in huge letters in an arch. I had pictures of him underneath, it was my shrine to him. In fact, the whole room was covered in TT pictures. There were a few MX pictures, right next to a signed picture of James Whitham on his Durex-sponsored Suzuki from the TT. It was a lad's bedroom, with a bit of MX clobber on the floor here and there. Becky looked puzzled and asked me 'What's this? What's Joey?' I just smiled.

We became inseparable pretty quickly. It felt like we'd only been dating for five minutes when we were off on the ferry to the Dutch TT at Assen with my dad and my stepmum. I argued my case, saying I didn't want to go unless Becky could come too. They went nuts; we'd only been together for three months and she was only 14 at the time. My Dad had a real downer on Becky when we got together because he thought she was too young and that we'd repeat the same problems as he and my mum had.

Eventually, however, they agreed to speak to Becky's mum and dad. When I think about the fact that Becky was younger then than our son Ewan is now, it seems mad, absolutely crazy. It was unusual back then and I doubt it'd happen nowadays, but I was obsessed with racing and I'd found someone who was happy to become obsessed with it too for me. I didn't want to let that go and it was definitely worth the aggro I got from my dad.

The trip was a bit of a disaster though. Becky had never seen a family like mine in her life. My dad has a short fuse so it was only ever a matter of minutes before he was ranting and raving about something. Pam, my stepmum, was only eight weeks away from giving birth to Faye, my stepsister, and she also had a two-year-old on her hip in the form of Kurt, my younger stepbrother. She shouldn't have gone really, but she did and we made the best of it.

*

Back then I used to ride with my best mate, a lad called Bosh who had a Yamaha Fizzy 50. It was always quicker than my AP. His birthday came before mine and he traded up to a Suzuki RG125. Suddenly he could do 100mph and I was stuck on the AP50 doing 40 everywhere.

I couldn't wait to get a bigger bike and as soon as I could upgrade, I got a Yamaha TZR125. By this stage, I'd pretty much had enough of motocross and I traded in my Suzuki RM125 for it. I'd reached a level on the RM where I didn't think I was ever going to get any better so it was time to change it. The hardest thing about stepping away from MX was telling my dad that my heart wasn't in the job. I think he was pretty wounded when I told him what I wanted to do with the RM. At the same time, he was a biker himself so there was no way he was going to hold me back.

I took the RM to Vin Duckett's in Blackpool and we did a deal. I actually went in looking for a different model of TZR – I wanted the one with the speed blocks along the side – but when I got to the shop they didn't have the one I wanted. I was desperate for a new bike and I had to have one that day so I took the only one they had. The paintwork used to piss me off but I loved that 125. I used to ride it flat out absolutely everywhere in jeans and trainers. Licence plate F589 TFV. I was the king on that bike, nobody could get anywhere near me. I didn't just think I was Joey Dunlop when I rode it; I thought I was Joey, Schwantz and Lawson all rolled into one, I pretended to be all of them. I thought I was a world champion every time I got on it.

Out of the box, the TZR only made about 12 horsepower and had a maximum speed of around 70mph. We knocked the pin out of the electronic power valve and wedged the valve open. It made the bike fly, even if it made it run rough and gave it a very narrow powerband.

It sounds flash talking about having all these bikes around me, but I wasn't into anything else and didn't have a pot to piss in. Christ knows how I used to afford to keep fuel in the thing. That 125 felt like a race bike to me, mostly because my AP50 was pretty shit. With its 1970s technology, it was more like a scooter. Suddenly with the TZR I had a proper bike. It had disc brakes, clip-on bars, a screen and fairings, and made all the right noises. It looked like a motorbike! Suddenly I thought I was the man. I couldn't afford proper kit but I didn't really care. I've grown up now and wouldn't dream of taking the kind of risks I was happy to take back then, but they always felt calculated. Most of the time, anyway.

I hit a bull on the TZR once, out on the roads near my house. I came flying round a corner and there it was in the middle of the road. I whacked it with my left arm. It came up in a lump straight away, like something out of a Popeye cartoon. I didn't break the bone but I might as well have considering how much pain I was in. I rode home with my left arm in tatters, balanced on the tank. Another time I nipped out for a bottle of wine and stuffed it down my jacket. Then I decided to pull a wheelie. When I landed the wine smacked into the tank and dented it. I was fucking spewing. It's not even like there was anyone there to see the wheelie either.

*

The first time I rode Manx roads was on my TZR in 1989. I went with my mates, Bosh and Dobby, all of us on our 125s. It was complete carnage. I'd studied the circuit for years and felt like I knew every corner before I'd even turned a wheel on the island. I'd sat and watched, I'd listened on the radio, I'd read and dreamed about it for years. Finally, I was going to ride it.

As soon as we rode off the boat in Douglas we headed up to the paddock. We'd made a plan to camp as close to the racers as we could. We fully expected to be kicked out but I wanted to be right in there with the boys. I wanted to feel what the atmosphere of a TT race paddock was like. For some reason we were left alone so we pitched our tents on a dot of grass behind the pits. I doubt I'd even packed a spare pair of underpants. Just jeans, trainers, a paddock jacket and my Arai helmet, which I'd painted in Mat Oxley replica colours after somebody had run over it at a petrol station. I had to use filler to hide the massive dent and it was about as much use as tits on a fish by the time I'd finished painting it. I wasn't really a fan of the Mat Oxley colours either, it just ended up being the style I chose.

Within half an hour of leaving the boat, we'd dumped our kit and I was riding the course for the first time. Those roads were the Holy Grail for me and the feelings of freedom and speed were incredible. Handily, parts of the course also felt like the roads I was used to riding at home. I was always a bit quicker than the boys I was riding with, maybe took a few more risks or whatever, but it was heaven finally to be able to go properly fast in the zones where there were no speed limits. We did 30mph in the 30 limits, stuck to 40 in the 40 zones and when we got to the first section where you could ride as fast as you like, I went flat out. As fast as that little 125 could carry me, in my jeans and trainers. I look back now and think that I was lucky to get away with it, but at the time all I wanted to do was ride as fast as possible.

I don't know how many laps I rode that first day. Every time it needed fuel I'd put some in and just crack on, going round and round the course again and again. I used to be able to get the thing off-clock coming down the mountain. I'd tell everyone it was 105mph but it was probably not even a ton.

I'd get up as early as I could on that trip to get an early lap in, have a bit of breakfast and go and watch the racing. Then as soon as the roads opened in the evening I was there on the TZR again, ready to get a few more cheeky laps in before the sun set. It felt like I was at a free racing track.

Mad Sunday was chaotic, just like it is now. I was up the inside of everyone and round the outside of everyone else. 1000s, 750s, whatever they were on, I was coming past them on that little 125. I used to treat everyone as competition and whoever was in front of me was going to get one. I'd stop at the Creg with everyone else, heart racing and mouth gibbering away at a million miles an hour, and guys would come over to rant at me for passing them too closely. 'You fucking lunatic! You mad little bastard, you'll end up killing yourself riding like that!' I had no idea. I liked it more when guys that I'd passed would come over and comment how quick my bike was for a 250. When I'd point out that it was only a 125 they'd die of embarrassment at being done by such a little bike.

On that first trip those first few laps were everything I'd hoped they'd be. As usual, I left wanting more, but this time, rather than wanting to sit on the bank and watch more racing, I wanted to ride more laps, add more speed and push myself harder round there. It was just as hard to see Douglas disappear out of sight on the ferry home as it had been the first time I went with my dad. I still get that feeling when I leave the place now, even after all these years.

*

Once I'd traded my RM125 for that TZR125 road bike I left MX behind for a bit. I came back to it for fun and would ride whatever I could get my hands on when I had the time to go and scramble at a local meeting. It'd scratch the itch while I wasn't road racing but that was about it. I know my limits and you've got to be pin-sharp all the time in MX. If you want to win, it's not the sort of thing you can just dip in and out of.

When I look back at those early days of MX racing, I think my dad just wanted me to be happy with my results, in much the same way that I want my son Ewan to be happy with whatever he's putting his effort into. His frustration shone through because he could see that I wasn't making the most of my opportunities. Soon enough I'd give my dad a chance to get his teeth into the next stage of my racing career, only by now I was too big for him to leave me in the back of the van if I bottled it.

*

I'd also started driving by this stage. I used to knock about in my mum and dad's cars whenever I could. I had four lessons and went for my test. I remember telling Becky on the day of my test that if I was outside school in a car when she came out, then I'd passed.

Sure enough, when she came out of school, there I was in my dad's black Renault Fuego. Insurance was easy as me and him share the same name. I'd get the odd pull by the police now and then, not that it mattered. Whenever I got a producer, I'd take the paperwork for the car to the police station, but it was all in my dad's name. Job done.

I can remember driving some real shit back then. Marinas, Avengers and old Mazda 626s. I'd fill them full of my mates and we'd be off, flat out everywhere burning fuel that they'd all chip in for.

None of the driving or riding that I'd done on the roads or on my MX bike was ever driven by aggression. I didn't feel the need to get angry to get past someone. I just thought I'd either be quicker than them or I wouldn't. I sometimes think my lack of aggression on the bike and my absence of fighting prowess come from seeing where those things got my dad. He's ended pretty much every job he's ever had with a slap for someone. One of the first jobs he had was as a saddle maker's apprentice. He copped a load of stick from one of the older guys there, I think it must have been because my dad has always been a bit of a chunker. Anyway, the guy kept ripping into him and it ended up with my dad laying him out.

When I was on the bricks as an apprentice, I used to get a bit of stick as well. It seemed to be the way back then for the young lads. I took it on the chin and let things slide. I suppose my dad just looked at these situations differently from me. The last job he had was as a taxi driver and even that one ended with him giving another driver the good news one day. It's not like he's some kind of monster. Some people just deal with things differently from others. He's still my dad and I have nothing but respect and love for him. Everybody who knows him has an affectionate story to tell about him. Even if they got bullied by him back in the 1970s, they can look back and laugh at it now because he's not the kind of guy to bear a grudge and let these things linger.

*

When my mum and dad eventually divorced, this beautiful Kawasaki KR1S appeared for me. I've always referred to it as my divorce present from my mum and dad. I think my dad got it with the intention of riding it himself, but he knew I'd be itching to get on the thing. I did my test at Belle Vue in Manchester on a Honda CG125. It cost about £90 to do one of the first ever two-part tests to ride a full power bike. My dad took me to do Part One and when the Part Two bit came through the post a few weeks later, I was straight back to the test centre because the KR1S was waiting. I borrowed a mate's 125 Aprilia to get there and that afternoon I was out on the Kawasaki.

The day after my test, we were going to the TT. The boat was booked. So I put myself under loads of pressure to pass the test, knowing that if I failed I wouldn't be able to ride the 250. Obviously, I passed with no problems and Becky and me were on the boat the next day. Within 24 hours of my bike test, I was riding my KR1S flat out on the roads around the Isle of Man TT course, like I used to ride around Morecambe with Becky on the back.

I can't even remember how we got the bike across the first time. It must have been some kind of blag. We'd have slept on the floor of a mate's hotel room in Port Erin. I didn't have a shilling in my pocket but I didn't care, I just wanted to be there and watch the racing. The Isle of Man is a magical place and those were amazing days.

*

While I was on that trip, my Nana fell down the stairs, setting off a downward spiral with her health. She took a fair bump and then couldn't get herself up off the floor. She never really got over it and ended up with pneumonia. She moved her bedroom downstairs for a while but eventually had to go into a home. I've always felt responsible because I wasn't there to help her up when she fell.

When we realised that she'd have to go into a home, I moved across the road and into Becky's house with her family. Becky still tells me that this was because I was a wuss and didn't want to live on my own across the road. She knows me very well ...

It was a big deal, being allowed to live in their house. We'd only been dating for about eight months but Becky's mum and dad, Steph and Dick, said they loved me to bits and that I should move in.

It was a three-bedroom council house which already had four kids in it. Becky has two sisters, Ruth who was eight and Rachel who was 14, and a brother Richard who was two when I moved in. I got on really well with them all from day one and still do now. They looked around for somewhere for me to sleep and it ended up being the sofa. So that where I slept for a few years. Apart from when I used to sneak into Becky's bed, back in the days when we could both fit in a single bed.

I don't think I knew when I first started dating Becky that things were going to get as serious as they did. I remember hearing about girls getting pregnant at 13 when I was at school, but we'd been dating for 18 months before I drilled her. We were both virgins and didn't really know what we were doing in that department. Looking back, I'm glad I wasn't too sure what I was doing because of the age gap. Perhaps I wasn't quite a full paedo, just a semi-one.

I'd never really had any other birds in my life and had no idea where the future was going to take us. I just wanted to race bikes. Becky went to college and learned to be a nursery nurse. She worked in various nurseries, grafted away for a long time and was always ready to chip money into the racing pot for me to make things better. Our lives were very different from the ones that normal kids dating at our age would lead, but more exciting.

CHAPTER 6

The Racing Buzz

WE'VE ALL SAT and daydreamed about what we want to be when we leave school and how we might get there, but it's best to have a fall-back plan, just in case. My dad told me that I'd need a trade, something to pay the bills. It's not like I sat and had a conversation with him where I said I'd like to be a road racer and we came up with a plan. It was more about having a skill that I could use anywhere I needed to earn a living. I think my dad talked me into the idea of being a bricklayer because he'd had the experience of losing the lot when the garage he worked so hard to build went down the pan. He didn't want me to end up going down the same route.

My love was for bikes, so going to college and learning something I wasn't interested in was tough. But I enrolled on an apprentice bricklaying course anyway and got stuck in. It took a couple of years and I qualified in 1990. I took it seriously and worked hard, but I hated it. It just felt like I was lining myself up for a lifetime of holding a trowel and chucking muck at bricks. It was fun in a way though, mostly because I was riding to and from college on the KR1. I knew it would be good for me to meet new people and having a trade made sense, so I knew if I stuck at it I'd eventually see light at the end of the tunnel. But it was always in the back of my mind that racing was there for me to work towards as well.

Because I was working on an apprenticeship scheme, I was only paid about 50 quid a week but I was expected to do the work of a grown man. So I resented the job from the off. I know it's part of growing up, but when you're getting picked up at quarter to seven in the morning and you have to ride to work in the back of a fag-smoke-filled van, sitting on a bag of cement listening to men arguing about football when all you want to do is go racing, you begin to question where you're going in life. I used to look at top-level racers in MCN and wonder how I could be more like them and achieve what they had. Meanwhile, I used to look at the guys on the building site and try and figure out what I had to do to not be like them. I don't mean that in a bad way. I didn't think I was better than them, I just didn't fancy spending my life doing the same thing as them.

Maggie Thatcher screwed the job for builders everywhere around that time and the recession hit us hard. I can remember how it all came crashing down. I was working on Heysham Heliport at the time, the platform used to ferry guys out to the rigs. The boss

Tyrone Lewis came up to me one day and just said that he had no more work for me. I was screwed and had to start scratching round looking for work.

I worked for a builder called Mick Stainton, who was very professional. He ran a bigger and better outfit, and did real quality work. I still feel proud of the houses we built when I drive past them in Morecambe. But it was a difficult time to be a tradesman and all I was interested in doing was being a bike racer. I still look at people doing those jobs and wonder if they're enjoying them. What's in their heads all day? I know I enjoyed bits and pieces of the work I did when I was a brickie but there is no way on earth that I could ever see myself doing it forever. I still see some of the guys that I used to work with round town.

One day I was driving to a bike event and saw a guy that had knocked me for a few quid back when I was laying bricks. He'd treated me like shit and then not paid me. I'd worked at a university for him for two weeks and when it was payday I asked him to square me up with my money. He just looked at me and said 'Nah, I can't pay you.' He was older than me and I didn't have a leg to stand on. I tucked my tail between my legs and set off for home with my tools, but I hated being treated that way. I'm not the first person that has ever happened to and I'm sure I won't be the last, but it really hurt. Anyway, years later, there he was, waiting to cross the road in front of me with his bucket of tools on his arm. I immediately remembered how shit it felt that day. So what did I do? I stopped the car, flashed my lights so he could cross the road and give him a wave as he went by with his bucket and trowel hanging off his arm. I was in my Porsche 911, bought and paid for with the money I'd earned racing bikes and he was still laying bricks in the cold. I gave him a toot on the horn and a cheery wave as he walked across the road in front of me. As anyone who knows me will tell you, I'm not spiteful.

*

While all this was going on, everyone at home was convinced I was going to die on the roads because of how fast things were getting on the Kawasaki. But they were also saying how quick I was and that I had to go racing to see if I was any good. I started having a proper think about it but it just felt like we couldn't afford it.

The Kawasaki was a massive step up from the 125, but I was on it and I was gone. This was a proper 130mph bike. Perimeter frame, four-pot calipers, it had everything. It was like a racing bike with lights on and I was fast on it. I'm not trying to be a smartarse but I was never out of shape on it. Don't get me wrong, I was an idiot, always doing wheelies with Becky on the back and usually going far too fast. But in my world, I was in complete control. Everything felt like a race, so it had to be full gas everywhere and I had to win, even if there was nobody else on the road. I used to ride with lads on bigger bikes and always felt like I had to get into their ribs and get past them.

We were all pretty handy riders in the gang that I used to ride with. There would be two or three of us that would get away from everyone else but in my mind we were fast and safe. I'd always be prepared to try a bit harder than the others. It didn't matter if we were on different bikes; I liked to be at the front. I'd spent most of my time on the AP50 riding on my own, racing the road and myself. On the TZR 125 it was all about being quicker than the lads I used to ride with and always trying to go flat out. By the time I got on the 250 KR1S, I felt like I could nail anything on the road, not just my mates. I could smoke everybody on that thing. Exups and Genesis Yamahas, Honda VFRs, anything I came across was getting overtaken. I was definitely going fast.

I spoke to my dad about TT racing but it didn't look as though it was going to happen. We just couldn't afford it for a start. And Dad wanted me to race but he definitely didn't want me to go road racing. He'd never really pushed me into motocross; it was just something for him to get his teeth into, something to stimulate him. He loved working on bikes, being surrounded by engines and getting stuck in. He used to love chucking a new piston in my RM for me and getting it set up just right. I wanted to be a successful racer and have something I could make a career out of and I couldn't see that happening through motocross. I didn't want to be a bricklayer all my life and it looked at the time like they were my only options workwise.

When we look back and talk about my racing career now, my dad always maintains that I've not got that killer instinct in me, which is why I'm a lot better racing the roads than grids full of guys on short circuits. Motocross needed complete dedication, plus killer instinct. Dad and Becky say I'm the first one to roll over in a head-to-head situation with another racer going into a hairpin or something tight. Like I've never wanted to put myself in a position where I'm not leaving myself enough room to still be safe. I was chatting about this at Macau in 2016 and somebody politely pointed out that this is why I'm still here today. It makes sense to me.

I'm not saying I'm not a calculated racer and it gets frustrating when people say I'm only good on the roads. I'm a good short-circuit racer. When I won the British 250 championship, I had five pole positions, qualified on the front row of every single race and stood on the podium every time. I only had two wins, but I won the championship and I only fell off once all year.

Maybe I've got it wrong and I've always been a lunatic, like some people used to think when I was riding on the roads with my mates. Public roads are obviously not controlled environments and something could have pulled out on me at any moment, but I knew all the roads round my way like the back of my hand. I still do. Every bump and drain, every kink and crest. There's nothing to say I couldn't have come over a crest and hit something in the road. It happened to good friends of mine and they got hurt and moved on from bikes because of it. But riding fast on the roads back then was a passion, like a drug. I had to do it

*

I'd only been riding the 250 for three months when my old man got sick of being told how fast I'd been riding. He came up to me one day, grabbed me by the shirt and said, 'So, you think you're good enough to race do you?' Like I said, I wasn't much of a tough guy, but I've always been a gobby little shit so I just said yes. I'm not sure if he thought that I'd bottle it and say no.

If my dad hadn't called me out, I have absolutely no doubt that I would have killed myself, and probably Becky too. We were just kids and had no idea of the dangers. We'd be flat out on that thing everywhere, genuinely flat out, two up, Becky's hair waving in the wind and me racing my own shadow.

We made a plan to enter a race at Aintree. The circuit is only 60 miles away from Morecambe so it wasn't hard to get to. It's quite a cool track actually, it had hosted the British F1 Grand Prix in the 1950s and Geoff Duke had won there about the same time. It's pretty flat and is only about a mile and a half in length. I'd be amazed if there's more than five corners all the way round, so absolutely nothing like the TT. I entered the last round of the Aintree MCRC championship without a single fucking clue what was going on. Obviously I'd been around paddocks before when my dad was racing and during my time in MX, but as usual I was shitting it when the time came to pull on my lid and get on with the job.

The bike preparation we did was a comedy effort. I think we just took the lights and indicators off and that was that. I left the standard road-ready Dunlop tyres on and the bike was pretty much the same spec as it had been the day before when I was riding it round Morecambe. I took the number plate off and thought I was ready to show the world what John McGuinness was all about. I got demolished in the race. You'd think with only having five and a bit corners to remember that I'd have got my eye in quite quickly and be telling you how in my first race I blitzed everyone and made it clear that I was destined for greatness. Bullshit. I came dead last and was beaten to a pulp by everyone on the track, including two women. It was great to feel the buzz of racing the KR1S, but I hated being so far off the pace. Still, I knew I had much more in me and just set my sights on getting faster on-track and better at being prepared for racing off it.

*

So from then on, every penny I earned went in the racing pot. I didn't care about anything else. I just wanted to do as much racing as I could. I went to Darley Moor, Pembrey, all the way down to Lydden, Cadwell and anywhere else I could go to get a run out on my KR1S.

At the same time I entered the Superteens Championship, which was getting us into the British paddock. I was at the same race meetings as the Superbike rock stars: John Reynolds, James Whitham and all the others. It was all helping to guide me towards something bigger and better.

The first time I met David Jefferies was when we did Superteens in 1991. He intrigued me because he came from a famous racing family. David's dad, Tony, was a TT winner, as was his uncle Nick. They had bike shops and were doing well for themselves. I just thought Dave was a cool kid. He had an American motorhome and there weren't that many of them about at the time, I thought it looked really trick. I really wanted to have a look in the motorhome and was happy that Dave and me seemed to get along. Eventually we got quite pally and we used to have a bit of a craic together. Of course I managed to get a look in the motorhome as well.

We were in it at Brands Hatch having a brew and I asked him what the deal with the TT was. He told me flat he was never going to do it. He just didn't seem interested in it. I suppose I was and we talked about it a bit more, but we were only 18 or 19 years old. I don't suppose either of us thought for one second that we'd actually end up there, let alone having the success that we did.

Dave had a very distinctive riding style and he was fast. He could get his knee down in a straight line and seemed to have so much natural feel for what a bike was doing underneath him. Sliding bikes around seemed effortless to him and he could throw his hand to anything. He'd do a hill climb at Scarborough on a BMW GS and beat everyone. Then he'd jump on a trials bike and go well, or he'd climb on an MX and be fast straight away. There was just something about him that seemed to gel with any kind of bike.

It was all so easy to Dave, he just did it with natural ability, of which he had tons. He liked a pie, he liked pizza and he liked his chips. As a result I'm not sure if he had the right image for sponsors but I don't want to speak ill of the dead. He still got to ride at Grand Prix level though, when he replaced Peter Graves. He also had a go in World Superbikes on the Revé Kawasaki with John Reynolds, and he did some really cool stuff. I don't know if the TT was really on his radar and he was just playing at these other things.

*

I finished seventh in the Superteens championship that year, and it finally felt like I was making steps in the right direction. 1990 and 1991 were all about finding my feet and getting quicker as a racer. They were also about struggling and doing whatever I could to go racing, despite having no money. We used to get to the races in an old Renault Traffic with a caravan on the back. I swapped my first car for it. There wasn't a tax disc or an insurance certificate in sight.

By this time, my dad was working on the oil rigs, spinning spanners. He'd leave enough money for us to pay race entry fees before he went offshore and my mum would chuck a few quid's worth of diesel in the van. I'd have the 50-odd quid that bricklaying had paid that week and we were off. Nicking fuel from work, pinching food out the cupboards to go in the caravan, we did whatever we needed to do to go racing.

When my dad could make it to my races, he showed a lot of the old angry side that he'd displayed back when I was racing the RM125. I remember riding into the side of somebody going into the hairpin at Cadwell. I was still a novice racer but thought I was Jack the Lad. It was the first lap of practice on the club track layout that they don't use anymore. Going into the hairpin I leaned on a lad called Ian Sampher and down he went. I ended up running off the track, hitting the tyrewall and flying over it. My face was cut to bits. I looked up and my old fella was bounding towards me. He'd climbed under the fence and was coming for me down the track, while bikes were still riding around us. Red flags waving, smashed KR1S bodywork all over the place and all I could hear was him bellowing, 'Fucking hell!'

He grabbed the poor lad that I'd hit and was calling him a wanker. I was screaming at my dad to leave him, telling him it was my fault. He stormed off the track yelling fucks at me and everyone else. We didn't have a spare lever or cable so that was us on our way home before the weekend had even got going. Another stony, silent ride home in the van while he drove along in a foul mood.

It sounds hilarious now, going racing with my schoolgirl girlfriend and my mum for a team, but we made it work as best we could. That's the kind of commitment to me and my racing that my mum showed. Later on, when I was racing at the TT, she was always there to see me set off. I can't even begin to think about how it feels to see your child setting off at that place, but she's seen me go in pretty much every single race. Sometimes she'd just appear in the paddock after travelling across on her own. She didn't make a fuss, she just wanted to be there for me and I'll always love her for that support.

When my dad was working offshore, we would arrange to talk to each other about the bike and how it was handling so that he could help me even though he wasn't there. I'd have to wait by the phone box at the circuit for him to ring from whatever rig he was working on. No mobile phones or laptops back then, it was a notes-on-a-piece-of-paper and payphone job. I'd tell him about the gearing or whatever and he'd help me out.

The problem was I was only about 18 at the time and only had limited knowledge when it came to working on the bike. I used to leave things alone a lot of the time for fear of not being able to put them back together on my own. Two-strokes need constant fettling though, they have to be pulled apart all the time to make sure everything is how it should be. Jets need checking and all the rest of it. I spent a lot of time with my fingers crossed, hoping the bike would hold together for the race so that I could get it home for my dad to sort out when he got back from being away at work. I was getting quicker though, so something was working.

*

My Nana died when I was 18 and hadn't been racing long. I was at a race meeting at Cadwell with my dad, who didn't tell me that she'd passed away in the night. Dad chose to take me racing anyway. I fell off and he was mad as fuck at me, he just exploded and was way angrier than usual. He disappeared off into the car park to pinch a foot peg off someone's bike. It wasn't just that we just didn't have any spares, we had nothing. Diddly squat. Anyway, he nicked a peg and we carried on racing.

I think he always regrets not telling me straight away, but looking back I think he just wanted to block everything out so I could have a good day's racing and get a decent result for my Nana. On the way home he told me she'd died. It was tough. She knew I'd started racing but I was only a novice back then, with my orange jacket on out there on the short circuits. I just hope that if she's around me now, or up there or an angel or something, she's looking down on me and is happy. She was my biggest fan and it'd be mint for her to see me win, to know that I've achieved all this. Bless her. I still think about her quite a bit. I'm pretty hard-faced when it comes to death and tend to just think people should get over it. I got over her death, but at the same time, I've never been to her grave. Although Granddad Tommy was at my Nana's funeral, I've always thought that he'd died before her. There was nothing behind his eyes and he was gone a long time before his body gave up. I remember Nana how she was before I went to the

Isle of Man, before she fell down the stairs. She was just my Nana and she was ace.

*

Those times that we spent in the paddock with nothing to our names felt pretty normal. I think the majority of people there were on the bones of their arses, grafting away on the breadline and just about scraping enough to have some fun club racing at the weekends. It was different to how it is now. I know club racers now that are set up for a weekend's racing by Friday morning. That means leaving work on a Wednesday. The normal thing back then was to work until you knocked off on a Friday and get set up at the track early doors on Saturday morning. We couldn't really afford to go racing at all, let alone to take extra time off work to do it.

Of course, there were some bigger set-ups in the paddock, one or two lads whose parents had a few quid, which meant they had everything they needed. I didn't hold it against them. I always wanted a nice truck and somewhere warm to sleep, but rather than wasting my time hating these guys, I used to question why they had things that I didn't and think about what I would have to do to be able to have the same as them.

CHAPTER 7

Bobby's Helmet

I NICKED A few decent results in 1990, managed to stop finishing in the second half of the pack and moved up to the sharp end. I stumbled into the British Clubman's Championship in 1991. That was the first proper championship I got stuck into. Someone had seen me go all right at a smaller track, Aintree I think, and they said I should enter this Clubman's Championship race at Mallory Park. I didn't know if I'd be any good and I didn't have a clue what the series was about. I went along to the first round at Mallory. It was a rainy, shitty day but I didn't care about the weather and just blitzed everyone. Nailed them all and left the track leading the Championship. I went from winning club races to leading a National Championship in one go and it felt great. We decided there and then that I should do the full Championship.

One of the races was all the way down on the south coast at Lydden Hill raceway, about as close to France as you can get without getting wet. We set off in our

Renault Traffic van with a caravan hanging off the back of it. The old Renault was hard work and I used to have to drive it so steady. When we went uphill it used to get really hot. I was constantly driving it with one eye on the gauges. Eventually it blew up on the way down to Lydden and we had no idea how we were going to get home. In the end, I nursed it to a Shell station forecourt and joined the AA on the Friday. I handed over 65 quid and we got a temporary membership number. I limped the van to the track and then rang them the next day and said that I'd broken down. 'No problem sir' they said. They put the Renault on the back of a flat-bed truck, hooked up the caravan and towed us all the way back to Morecambe.

*

During the season I was using Shell oils, and if you won a race they'd give you a star to put on your bike. Then, in the last round, I ended up nicking the Championship. Throughout the year, Shell looked at the field of racers and would choose someone at the end to award a scholarship. Jason Vincent won the first one, then I won it in 1992.

When I won that scholarship I thought I was going to be a world champion and that everything was going to be great. How little did I know ... I was so naïve, thought that job was a dream and that everything would be plain sailing from there on in. I didn't realise that you never stop working at it.

There was an awards ceremony that meant going down to London with my family. I was an apprentice brickie and had to borrow a suit from my boss. My mum went, along with my brother Andrew, my uncle David and his missus, and my dad. We ended up walking the streets in London for a bit. I can remember my mum went to cross the road and some smart arse in a Jag beeped his horn at her. You've got to remember we're a bunch of northerners here, out in the big city with not a clue what's going on. The guy in the Jag was going nuts because my mum had stepped in his way. He edged his car forward at her while he was hanging off the horn. As my mum stepped out of the road, my brother just toe ended the side of the Jag, wham! A massive kick in the wing. The guy's head went and he jumped out of the car ready to go nuts at someone.

Now, my uncle David is a feisty little bastard. He's only short, but he's a stocky little shit. Jag man was striding at him, shouting about this and that. Wallop! Uncle David gave him one and he was sparko on the pavement of some fancy street in the middle of London. He picked himself up and tried to carry on fighting.

While him and my uncle David had it out in the street, my little brother Andrew booted the life out of the Jaguar, walking round it pulling bits off it wherever he could get his hands around something. We jumped in a cab as sirens drew closer. The bloke was left standing in the street with a fat lip and a smashed-up car. You can't use your car as a battering ram against a woman and you can't expect the McGuinness family not to unite when it needs to. My uncle had a five-millimetre fuse at the best of times. Seeing his sister in bother was all the excuse he needed.

We went and collected the scholarship. There were top rally drivers and other car racing winners there and me. It was the first time I'd been interviewed properly and I gave a little speech on stage. As part of the deal, I'd won a ride for the year on a new Yamaha FZR400RR. I thought the world was about to land at my feet. How wrong I was. I was convinced teams would be queuing up to get me on board. But the phone never rang.

*

I was partnered with Sean Emmett for the 1992 season as part of the deal. He rode the 400 and a 600. A couple of years older than me, he was also test-riding bikes for *Fast Bikes* magazine at the time and he knew the ropes when it came to sorting sponsorship. My dad and me were tucked away up north and didn't have a clue about presenting ourselves to teams with any kind of pitch. It was my riding that was doing all the talking, basically.

I'd turn up to a race meeting in my rotten old Iveco truck and everything was laid on for me. When I say rotten, I mean absolutely hanging. But the FZR was prepared for me and I didn't have to pay a penny for tyres or fuel or anything. The scholarship even came with leathers, so I wore Frank Thomas. It was still tough though, really competitive. Jim Moodie, Colin Gable, Farmer and Mike Edwards were all on the pipe out there on track.

I was going okay but I'd been dumped right in the thick of it with some quality racers. I got a rude awakening. I knocked on the door of the top ten now and then, scoring the odd point, but I found it pretty tough. I did manage one podium in the Spring Cup at Castle Combe, then immediately fell off the next day at Thruxton. I went down so fast on my front that I burnt my bell end. I've still got a little scar on the end of my bobby's helmet and I've still got the leathers with a patch over the crotch where I had them repaired.

I also broke my scaphoid at Cadwell and spent 12 weeks in a cast. As a rider nowadays, you can be defiant with an injury like that; you want it screwed together now, you want that laser treatment so you can get back out on the bike. Back then when you walked in to the doctor, they'd rip you for riding round in circles on motorbikes. They'd sling a cast on you and tell you to come back in six weeks for a check-up. I thought I could live with that as I'd only miss one round of racing and I could get back into it. When I went back the doctor said it had to stay on for another six weeks and that was it, season finished. I'd only managed a few rounds and hadn't done very well.

*

By the time I was out of my cast, the season was over, but there used to be a one-off powerbike race at Brands and they let me ride a 600 at it. There was a few bob to be won, so I was up for it.

I spoke to Team Shell and asked them what the score was for the following year. They said, 'We're off GP racing with Sean, that's the end of the scholarship'. It was such a sinking feeling, knowing I'd had a bike and everything I needed given to me and hadn't done it or myself justice. We were a bit bitter about Shell and Harris Performance putting the entire budget into Emmett, and Shell pushing the majority of the available money at him over the season, giving me the minimum required for it to look like I was getting a good deal.

But it was a long time ago and looking back it was unfair of me to think like that. I wasn't doing any networking or pushing myself in PR terms to nail sponsors. Shoei gave me a brand new helmet as part of that deal and I remember feeling like it felt right to have this kit, but I had no idea what went on behind closed doors to make these kinds of deals happen. I just thought that turning up and riding the bike was going to be enough. I didn't understand.

*

That season had been a wake-up call. It also forced me to go into mussel fishing. The country had dipped into recession and there was no money in laying bricks, so I went fishing and mussel picking with Becky's dad, Dick Langley. In comparison to what I was used to making on the bricks, I was earning a fortune. With work on building sites pretty much dried up and me living at home with Becky and her family, it made sense for me to go to work with her dad. Dick was a well-respected fisherman in Morecambe, he was also my girlfriend's dad and my landlord. I wanted the money, but not as much as I wanted to keep things sweet with him.

Nobody likes getting out of a warm bed when it's still dark outside, do they? I know I don't. A normal day for me would start at four or five in the morning. I'd drag myself onto my feet, get washed and pull on a pair of Becky's woolly tights. All I could think about doing was keeping warm. Looking good didn't matter. Pants, tights and then a pair of long johns over the top. A T-shirt, a long-sleeved top and then a jumper over that. Anything that would keep the cold out would go on. Wiping sleep out of my eyes, pushing my feet into cold, thick boots and thinking about the job at hand while the world still slept never got any easier. Creeping out the door and heading off down the hill. It used to feel like it was only me, Becky's dad and sometimes a milkman on the whole planet.

It was only about three miles to the Promenade. We'd drive down in Dick's battered pick-up truck, him puffing a freshly rolled fag while I begged a sip of coffee out of his flask, which looked like he stored it on the seabed. it was always black and tasted like piss. I hated coffee but it was warm and I wasn't. Out of the truck, stamping my feet to warm up, blowing condensation through chilled hands, eager to get to work so that I could get my blood flowing.

Mussel meat is at its fattest in the winter, so that's the best time to be a picker. It was a tough game. Sometimes we'd be out there before daylight waiting to follow the tide out. The next day we'd start an hour later and the next day an hour after that, following the tide timings. It was tough, but it was good, doing four hours' work and coming away with cash in your pocket. Mussel picking needs a craam, which is basically a fancy rake. The teeth have to be so many millimetres apart and they have to be a certain shape. This is dictated by fishing laws, which are weird. A lot of it goes back to licences that have been handed down from generation to generation of families since the 1700s. You also have to have a riddle and a riddling permit and you can only catch certain sizes of mussel.

You sit and wait for the mussel beds to be exposed as the tide goes out. Mussels don't move, they just sit in the sand. You have to rake them into the riddle, pull the riddle into the nearest puddle of water, then you have to tread it with your feet and 'riddle' them – clean them – so they are ready to go in 50-kilo bags. The best thing to do is leave them alive on the beach for a couple of days before bagging them, then drag them off the beach on the tractor to be stacked.

The Dutch and the French love their mussels and they'd come on a Friday to buy them. The French would go for the small ones because they're poncey. The Dutch wanted the big meaty ones. Two types of customer meant we needed to catch two types of mussel from different beds. They used to come with fistfuls of cash and start haggling.

Becky's dad was a commercial fisherman so he'd do the talking, I was just cold and did what I was told. Dick was such a trustworthy bloke, a genuine fella. He never had a pot to piss in and could have said to me that he'd have two quid out of every six-quid bag that I filled but he didn't. He was fair to me and would divvy up what we'd made once we'd shifted the bags and that was that.

I'd get six quid a bag and I'd aim to do ten to 15 bags a day. You could be out at six in the morning and then back home by ten with money in your pocket and the rest of the day free to sort bikes, do some extra work or doss around. A hundred quid a day was possible.

You get big tides and neap tides. Neap tides are only small. Big tides dump more water in and take more water out in the same amount of time. When the tide ebbs out, it goes right out and the beds are exposed, but there are only certain types of big tide that you can harvest mussels from. On the neap tides, the water feels like it's trickling in and out. The flow's gentle and sometimes doesn't expose the mussel beds. On those neap tides, I'd jump on a Dutch fishing boat called the *Still Austria*. Dick and me would go up to Barrow and dredge on this 90-foot boat. It was ace. That thing was a beast. It could take 180 tons of mussels at a time. The principle was the same as for hand-picking, but on a massive scale. The dredger would fill sacks by the ton and trucks would take the catch away. I really enjoyed it. It was only a short period of my life though, with four of us working away on that boat and me as the young skivvy.

Dick was dead chilled, laid back. I suppose there was a part of me that wanted to prove I was worthy of going out with his daughter. He wasn't a man to mess with though. I gave him some lip one day and he cracked me, full on, flat out in the jaw. I was like, 'ooh, I won't

Two years old on my first bike, which had a sidecar. Riding it behind my mum and dad's house on Granville Road.

Outside McGuinness Motorcycles, aged four. Doing what I did while my dad worked away in the shop.

Eighteen months old, outside my gran and grandad's paper shop, on Alexander Road in Morecambe.

A shit haircut and out-of-date clothes. Ten-year-old John McGuinness didn't care about how he looked. Nothing much has changed.

Third-year chemistry class at Heysham
High, a subject I used to really enjoy.

Firebird Freestyler, the first bike I rode
to the Isle of Man. I did thousands of
miles on that BMX, always with this
stupid smile on my face.

Fifteen or sixteen years old, trying to impress my dad at Lorndhay in an AMCA scramble on the RM.

Trainers, paddock jacket and a fistful of revs: impressing everybody and nobody on the Kingsway council estate. Becky lived on one side of this road and my Nana on the other.

Sneaking a cuddle with my childhood sweetheart. Me and Becky in the kitchen of her mum and dad's house in 1989.

Becky's first trip away with my family. Five up in a four-door, carnage to Assen for the GP. #nonstopargument.

Getting some cheap Tenerife sun on my broken leg in 2000. We knew my leg was broken, but we didn't know Becky's belly was full of arms and legs.

Still Austria, the Dutch-built mussel dredger that I worked on with Becky's dad. I regularly puked on it and borrowed fuel off it for my race van.

All the gear and absolutely no idea. Eighteen years old, racing the KR1S at Elvington Airfield Circuit, with Becky cleaning my visor and my brother Andrew keeping us company.

1992 at Mallory Park. My first test on the Shell scholarship FZR400. Thought I had the world at my feet. I didn't.

Twenty-one years old, wearing Becky's jumper in my dad's front room. This was the picture I used to show potential sponsors. My Iveco van is slowly rotting away outside.

First long-haul trip: the 250 race at Daytona in '97. No overnight garage at the track meant the bike shared a room with us. Got drunk and got my ear pierced on this trip.

1998, finally stopped sleeping in the back of a van and got a caravan. All mod cons, felt like a palace.

'96 North West 200, wondering why I'm at the sharp end with Joey Dunlop.

My first TT. Orange bib on as I make the jump at Ballaugh Bridge. Went under the radar with a high number in practice week. On race day I was number 18.

First ever TT pit stop. Becky did my screen and Birdy hung around looking cool with my drink.

First podium, 1997. Stole the fastest lap and stood on the podium with my hero, Joey Dunlop. An unbelievable day's racing and an incredible man.

First TT win in 1999, stood on the podium with Jason Griffiths and the late Gavin Lee. A new 250 lap record on a cracking bike, it was my time to shine and I did.

do that again'. I respected him for that and there was no retaliation from me. I was living in his house for nowt, dating his daughter and sharing a room when we were young, and they trusted me. I had a brilliant relationship with Becky's dad right up until he died and I still have a great relationship with her mum. I think I earned my respect from him. I worked hard and we worked well together. He'd probably never have said that to me though.

We used to fish for salmon and shrimps in Morecambe Bay. Shrimp in the day meant trawling and then at night we'd go salmon fishing in the boat. Then it'd be elvers (baby eels). There was a certain set of tides at a certain time of the year when the elvers would come. The life of an eel is tough and it doesn't get much better once they're caught. The baby eels would go to Japan. We'd get 260 quid a kilo and a kilo was a big handful.

Everything had to be right. You could only catch them at night, during particular tides and in the right kind of weather. You'd sit all night with a dip net. Sometimes you'd get nothing. When the tide was flooding (on the way in), the elvers would get washed in with it – hopefully into your net. Then when the tide was ebbing off, they'd come out round the sides, so you'd get two chances to catch on each tide. Some nights you could make 1200 quid and others you could come home empty handed.

We'd sit with a flask in the dark, talking and having craic. Dick was always looking to stitch me up. I remember one night we were out in a small salmon fishing boat. Dick jumped over the side to pull the boat along and told me to do the same on my side. He knew we were right on the edge of a shelf and I went straight off it. Down I went, waders filling with water while Dick pissed his pants laughing at me. We worked together for three good years, '93, '94 and '95. It wasn't my only job though. I used to do a bit of delivery driving for a hire company as well, every penny as always going straight in the racing pot.

All that money I was earning from the mussels was going into racing but it still wasn't enough to get me to every race. I'd do a round, miss a round, do what I could to race when I could. Like the old days when I was racing MX as a kid, there wasn't much of a plan, or what there was revolved around money. If I had enough we were going racing, simple as that. If I didn't have enough, I knew that I'd have to roll up my sleeves and earn some.

*

In 1993 I managed to save enough money to buy the championship-winning Yamaha TZ250 that Paul Marra Brown had ridden. My thinking was simple: if he'd won races and a championship on it, then I'd win races and a

British Championship on it too. When I bought it, I took a bag with seven grand in cash in it. It was an old-school moneybag like the ones you see in the movies with a dollar sign on the side. I plonked it down on the table in front of Rob Mac (who owned the bike) like some millionaire closing a deal. When I asked for the spares that came with the bike, the boys pulled out an old sprocket and a clutch lever. I'd been promised a couple of boxes of bits and pieces with the bike and thought I'd been done over on the deal. It was only when I was heading for the door to go home that they burst out laughing and pulled out a load of spares from under the table.

To make TZs go well you had to throw pistons at them all the time; new reed valves, plugs and plug caps, the lot. We didn't have any of that. In fact, we didn't have much of anything once we'd rattled through the spares that came with the bike. We were absolutely winging it from week to week. When we could afford it, we'd put some bits in it and results would improve. But the depth of field in those 250 races was unreal. It was bloody hard and there were some great riders out there, on good bikes run by good teams. We were learning though. It was a process we had to go through, just being out there doing the laps. I finished the 1993 British Championship in 31st place.

People used to ask us why we were wasting our time. One of my dad's mates offered to put some money in if we went back to club racing, where we'd no doubt be competitive. The way I looked at it, while I'd be winning club races, I wouldn't be learning anything. I needed to be part of that bigger picture so that's why I kept on pushing in the British Championship. I spent years under the radar, and then it felt like my career went off like a rocket. British Superteens, Clubman's Championship and a scholarship, wallop! Then I was back down the bottom again, running mid-pack at best when I stepped up to British Championship level. That would probably have been a good time to say 'Well, I've had a good go, maybe it's time to go and do something else.' But I didn't. I think what kept me at it was having had nothing when I was growing up, living on Becky's sofa with nothing to my name. I didn't care what I looked like or where I lived though, I just seemed to be driven by this passion for speed, racing and success.

*

At this time in the early 1990s a lot of my mates were getting into the rave scene. They were out every weekend at acid house parties and stuff. While they were trying ecstasy and driving round the country in a Vauxhall Nova dripped up to death with wide wheels and spoilers looking for a party, I was at home trying to keep my race truck on the road. As long as I had the van I had a way to get to the racing. It wasn't just a case of that being all that I could afford. It was all that I wanted.

The Iveco truck we used to run was a complete death trap. I crashed it into Knutsford Services once. We were on our way to Snetterton in the pissing rain with the TZ and a few old spares in the back. Becky was in the middle and a mate was on the other side. I started to get a whiff of neat diesel. I asked them if they could smell it. I pulled off at Knutsford to have a look. The return line from the diesel pump was blocked and broken off. We were yet to discover that diesel had been pissing all over the chassis and the back end of the truck. When I went for the brakes on the way into the services, I immediately lost the back end at 60mph. Lock to lock in a five-ton truck on the way up the slip road. We were all screaming as I wrestled away with the thing. We entered the services backwards, hitting one of those Shell signs that sits on a spring-loaded base, it said 'Motorcyclists Welcome' on it. Then we hit a tree. I smashed the back end of the truck in and there were lights and glass and bits of bumper all over the road.

The van was full of red diesel, which we used to call 'Ribena'. It had no tax, no MOT, nothing, and we're sat facing the wrong way on the road into the services on the M6. I hit the tree so hard that it knocked the gear linkage off, so we were going nowhere. I leapt out and put the linkage back on before pulling a comedy

10-point turn to get facing the right way. I drove straight through the services, we pulled off at the next junction and headed straight for home with no backlights and the back doors hanging off. I was shitting myself the whole way, waiting for the police to catch up with me. It wasn't until we got home that I realised the bike was on its side and my kit was everywhere.

We had some good craic in that truck. I set Becky's legs on fire in it once. Her seat wasn't really a seat, more a perch over the engine underneath us in the cab. She told me there was smoke coming out of it while I was driving along, which I obviously ignored. Next thing there were flames coming out of the air vents where the heater fan had seized up. Becky had her feet on the dash and ended up kicking the windscreen out in a panic. It was so rotten that it didn't take much of a kick. We finished the rest of that journey with no glass. I fished a few helmets out the back and we drove on with the visors down and a gaping great hole where the windscreen used to be.

When I say we had nothing, I really do mean that we had not a thing. But it was brilliant fun, an ace craic looking back. The only thing I was worried about when we were driving about was hurting someone else on the road. Not having a tax disc didn't matter to me. I used to think to myself, 'This isn't right, but I'm not hurting anybody doing this so it's not morally wrong'. I just got on with it.

Another time Becky and me were heading to Croft and I popped one of her tits out in the truck when she fell asleep. There was a stack of road works on the motorway and we were crawling along. I was pointing the tit out to a load of lads working at the side of the road, they were laughing like fuck until she woke up and went absolutely mad at me.

I can remember us laughing a lot in that truck on the way to races. Sometimes it'd feel like we were out on a date, chatting away to each other as the motorway miles clocked up rather than sitting in a restaurant somewhere in Morecambe. It'd always end in some kind of scam though, like when I smuggled Becky into the Gold Cup at Scarborough. I told the man at the gate she was my younger sister and got her in for half price, which you had to be under 14 to get. That goes back to my dad and the times he used to stick me and my brother in the boot of whichever car he was knocking about in to save a quid when he wanted to watch the races. Clearly it rubbed off.

*

I entered a race at Donington Park on the TZ which ended in tears when I decided to have a crack at my dad. I blew the crank in practice. It was a couple of years old and was pretty tired. We were scrimping our way through racing as per usual. I used to climb in the Dunlop tyre bin at the track and fish out usable rubber that had been thrown away. People in the paddock would give me the odd spark plug and other bits and pieces that were worn out to them but better than anything I had in the back of the Iveco Deathtrap.

Dad was screaming at me for blowing it up again while he was pulling the motor apart. I had a moment of madness and decided I was going to belt him one. Smack! I punched him as hard as I could right in the side of his head. He barely winced and I immediately thought, 'Oh shit, I'm in for it now'. I hadn't thought about my escape route and had to squeeze past him to get away. He got up and gave me one back, I went flying through the side of the awning, with everyone in the paddock watching. He was still screaming at me while I ran off crying, leaving Becky to console little Kurt, who by this time was also in tears.

We've had our fights for sure, but it was always a good craic. I get on great with my dad now, he's ace. He's funny as fuck and we always have a laugh whatever we're doing together. He's 65 and full of tales of the stuff he's done over the years. I need to get him out a bit more. He didn't go to the TT in 2016, for the first time in ages. He'd had a hip replacement and was whining about it. I thought his hip would be just as sore at home as it would at the Isle of Man. It's not like it would have hurt any more sat at the side of the road in a deckchair with a radio and a programme in his hand. I'm sure he'll be back for more in 2017.

*

I kept struggling on, nicking the odd point here and there. Thirty-first place in 1993 turned into 26th in 1994 which turned into 16th in 1995. I didn't want to give in and felt like I was making progress in the right direction. Working with Becky's dad all the while was brilliant and there was cash to be earned. My dad would help, everyone would help and we'd go racing. But however you want to look at it, those days racing in the early to mid-nineties were my reality check. I came into racing thinking I was going to change the world. Back then the world wasn't ready for changing and every point I scraped was hard to earn.

CHAPTER 8

Robbed at the North West

WHEN I ANNOUNCED to my dad in 1994 that I was going road racing and had entered the North West 200, he told me he wanted nothing to do with it. He went fucking mad at me because I wanted to road race. When I look back now it's hard for me to think that he was surprised. I'd grown up watching road racing and was getting quicker on the TZ. It felt like the natural thing to do. We argued and he shouted that if I wanted to go I'd have to go on my own. I said, 'Fuck you, I will!'. So I did. Now I'm a parent, I can see why he said and did what he did. Road racing is obviously far more dangerous than short circuit stuff and I suppose he was just trying to keep me safe. I do wonder if he shouldn't have thought of that before propping me up in the grass at Bray Hill back when I was ten years old though.

To get to the North West and race it properly, I needed help, but I ended up going with just Becky. In a way, getting there was as much fun and drama as the races themselves. I did the whole thing on a wing and a prayer.

Bike prep, packing the knackered Iveco van without any real spares for the bike and then finally getting out in the race. We did all of that the hard way. Aside from the parts where I pulled my helmet on and rode the bike, Becky was there by my side all the way.

The van was full of red diesel as usual. Becky's dad used to give me the nod on when I could sneak up to the boat and steal the Ribena out of it to put in the van to go racing. I'd syphon it out the boat into jerry cans and away we'd go, still no tax or insurance. It was so hard to drive that nobody else could figure out how to change gear. Everything on it was broken or about to break. The windscreen wipers didn't work for three years.

The troubles in Ireland were still bubbling then and I remember being stopped at roadblocks and questioned about where I was going. I was shitting myself even getting there, let alone racing.

All my kit was knackered, not just the van. The bike was tired and we just didn't have enough parts or the cash to refresh it. The clutch had started slipping by the second race and while I can now see the value of all the learning and character building, at the time it pissed me off that we put all that effort into getting there but I couldn't seem to get a result that would do us justice.

We'd scrimped whatever cash we could pull together to be there and when we arrived, I had a count up and had about 90 quid in my pocket. While we were out mooching round the pits one day, somebody climbed into our van, went through the pockets of my jeans and stole the money, putting my jeans back where they'd found them. We were well and truly fucked. I went to the organisers and told them that I couldn't get home because all my money and been stolen. Billy Nutt and Mervyn White gave me enough cash to get home. Can I see Stuart Higgs or Palmer doing that for a younger me? I doubt it. I still can't quite believe that we got there, let alone got home. We did and although there was no Champagne spraying, I'd managed to make the transition from short circuit racer to road racer.

*

Back in the 250 British Championship I was still plugging away. My results were moving in the right direction, but it was in 1995 that I got what I'd class as my first break in racing. I had a look at who was sponsoring who locally, so that I could try to figure out how to get a deal that would help me. I used to go and tug on Paul Bird's shirt and remind him I was there, as I knew him a bit from the scrambling scene, where he'd sponsored Chris Palmer and Steve Patrickson. I never nailed it because I wasn't very good at selling myself back then.

One of Birdy's mates was a bloke called SM. His real name was Steve something or other. He'd travel from Penrith to all the races and he was a good bloke. He lived on his own, had no bird and a good job, so he had a load of money. He came up to me one day in the paddock and gave me 250 quid, so I bought some new pistons for the bike. It was three years old and crying out for spares at the best of times. New pistons couldn't have come along at a better time and made the motor feel quite fresh again. Next time out at Donington I went really well, finished near the top ten and in the points. I think that was one of the turning points. SM and Birdy were mates and I'd finally caught Birdy's eye.

The British 250cc championship was so hard. From the top to the bottom of the grid there were good racers lining up every round. Nigel Bosworth, Steve Sawford and all those guys knew what they were doing. All of a sudden I'm riding round with some decent lads, getting past a few of them as well, all because my bike is a bit sharper thanks to some new pistons.

When we eventually put a deal together, Birdy wanted some money from me. I agreed despite not having a shilling to my name. He offered me a Honda RS250 but wanted ten grand. Back then I didn't even know what ten grand looked like. I just said I'd get it and thought I'd figure out where to find it later. He also wanted me to buy a truck as well, so I did. I had a tyre deal with Bridgestone and I had to pay my entry fees to race. I agreed to it all and decided to worry about finding the money another time.

I was about 23 and back laying bricks full time, earning about £250 a week. On the strength of a handshake I'd strapped myself up for the cost of a truck, all my race entry fees, plus ten grand. There was no contract. In return, Birdy supplied me with a brand new Honda RS250 plus spares.

The spanner man on the bike was a bloke called John Clucas, who did the work for free. He was a lad from Garstang who was friendly with everyone. He used to bring his missus to the racing and they seemed to really enjoy being in the paddock.

In 1996, thanks to Paul Bird, I didn't have a care in the world. I thought I'd find the ten grand he wanted, and if I couldn't I'd just go to plan B. I had no idea what plan B was though.

I put everything I had into getting an ex-Tuffnells 7.5-tonne truck, painted it up to look the part and was off. A couple of rounds into the season, I was getting myself into financial trouble. I wasn't winning any prize money and John Clucas was sticking the fuel bills on his credit card. I held my hands up to Birdy and told him that I was struggling to find a way to get hold of the money. I said I was going to have to throw in the towel in. Birdy being Birdy, came up with a solution that worked for everyone. He was honest with me and he was fair. We worked things out and I was happy, but we were still doing things on the cheap.

I ended up doing a bit of work at Frank Wrathall's engine shop. When I finished bricklaying for the day, I'd grab Becky and we'd head to Frank's place in Garstang so that I could work on my race bike engine. We'd do all the prep work ourselves. I'd strip the motor down and clean it up, then Frank would check it all and put everything back together again. I did that for two years, working off the money I didn't have to put into the team.

At the time, my mum was working in a local pub called The George, and if we'd had a good week, Becky and me would go in there for a few beers and a game of darts with my mum. Mum would buy us a drink and the three of us would have a laugh together. Despite the hard times, my mum was always there to help us however she could. She'd do anything for me, chip in when we needed a few quid for racing or buy the beers in the pub when we'd spent what we had on bits for the bike. I love her to bits and will always be grateful for what she sacrificed for me, there's no way I'd be doing what I'm doing now if she hadn't helped back then.

CHAPTER 9

TT Debut

THE FIRST TT race I did was in 1996. I was umming and ahhing about going. I wanted to but I didn't know how I was going to get there. All I had was a bike. That year I ran at the North West 200 in Northern Ireland and went really well. I rode at the front in the 250 race with Joey Dunlop, Woolsey Coulter, Owen McNally, John Creith and all the other top riders in the division. I realised that I might be pretty handy on the roads and asked Birdy if we should do the TT. The NW200 isn't long before the TT, so we didn't have much time to put a plan together, we just knew that I was going to go.

Looking back over the years, I've seen my path cross with Joey Dunlop's all along the way. Just the tiniest chance meetings here and there and my first TT race was no exception. I ended up taking Joey's bike in the van with mine. I picked it up from Frank Wrathall's tuning shop where it had been in for some work along with mine. I was asked if I could deliver it to him and his lads in the paddock, so I loaded into my van as carefully as I could, packing soft stuff around it to protect it. I noticed it had a tiny dent in the tank. It was from a crash he'd had at the Tandragee a week or so before. There it sat, my hero's bike, strapped down next to mine. I was bursting with pride having it in my truck. The truck also contained half a Wickes kitchen (not plumbed in, with a bowl under it), so you can imagine how bizarre it was to look in the back and see a Joey Dunlop race bike in there.

When I got to the Isle of Man I didn't have a garage or anywhere to stay. Mentally, I was ready to do it, but logistically, I was miles off. But I was back in my 7.5 tonner with a new bike in the rear and a few spares, and it felt like I was in the perfect place to start my TT career.

I got off the ferry at six in the morning in Douglas and it was a beautiful day. I asked a racer called Mick Lofthouse where he was staying. He told me he was at the Monaville hotel on the Promenade. I followed him there and parked up outside. He went in for a sleep and I had a kip in the cab of the truck. It was a boiling-hot morning so I wound the window down and stretched out across the three seats. He came out a bit later and chucked a bucket of water over me. Mick was a bit of a joker like that. Eileen and Billy, the hotel owners invited me in for a bit of breakfast and I ended up sharing a room with Mick. He'd followed me on the track a bit in the British championship. He was a smooth rider himself and told me I'd be ideal for the TT.

Riding round on that first practice session didn't feel any different from riding round anywhere else. I was excited to be there of course, and after the pace that I'd shown at the NW200 I thought I might do all right, but I definitely didn't ride onto the track feeling like I was going to suddenly dominate the whole thing. I've mentioned a few times how important I think it is to get some real experience under your belt before you go to that place. The fact that I was 24 by the time I raced there is testament to that. I'd waited years to get the chance to be a TT racer, to be one of those men who had blurred my ten-year-old vision when I was on the grass at Bray Hill back in 1982. I'd gradually built up to the point of getting there and knew that it would take time to get to a point where I could ride the place fast. That's what experience gives you, the realisation that you can't force the pace at the TT. Nobody can.

Practice week was difficult but I was enjoying myself. The weather was crappy so a lot of the practice sessions got delayed and then cancelled. Then on the last practice session on the Friday before race week, Mick Lofthouse was killed.

The guy who told me that I'd be all right there, who'd let me sleep in his room and held my hand a bit was gone. When I found out, I remember thinking, 'I'm not doing this.' I was ready to jump back in the truck and get back on the boat home there and then, Mick's dad,

Arthur, came across and told me to just get the first race done and make a decision on whether or not to come back afterwards. He said that Mick would have wanted me to race and that I should get out there and enjoy it. My head was in bits, but I decided to take his advice.

When I think back to the first MX race that my dad took me to, and how I was so nervous and scared of the unknown that I burst into tears before the flag had dropped, I'm amazed I even lined up for that first TT race. I think I just had to.

*

Race day was beautiful, the weather had come good and it was hot. The track was great and I had a pretty good race. Joey Dunlop won on the 250 that I'd delivered to him, Jim Moodie finished in second place and Jason Griffiths was third. I finished 15th, three seconds behind Richard Coates. Bruce Anstey also made his TT debut that year. I don't think anyone saw him coming either. I'm still not sure anyone understands Bruce, even now. There was also a top Welsh guy called Paul Owen who had his first time out. He deserves a mention, he was a cracking lad but he somehow seemed to miss the boat with opportunities.

Then there was David Jefferies. 1996 was also his debut year and he took to the TT like he took to everything else. He was fast straight away. He did the same at Scarborough, the North West, Macau and basically anywhere he chose to race. He ended up dominating the TT and really raised the bar in terms of lap times and big performances. That first year I got the best newcomer award in the 250 class – I was dead proud of the little trophy and still have it at home – but Dave got best newcomer overall. He ended doing the Senior on a 600 as well and got more laps in than I did, but I couldn't touch him anyway.

It felt like one minute you were flat out on the run down from the Creg and then suddenly it was all over and you were in the beer tent with fans and other racers, chatting away and thinking about which way you want to go with your TT career. After that race there was no way I wanted to go home. Robert Holden was killed on the same lap as Mick. It's not that we chose to forget about them, we just carried on. You harden yourself to it and death becomes something you deal with. Arthur Lofthouse had talked me into staying for that first 250 race after his son was killed, and after that I was hooked.

It's possible that I treat death and dying the way I have done over the years because my Nana died when I was still a young man. I think I was half prepared for her death, as she was always smoking fags and wheezing. She was knackered, the old girl. My generation went in for smoking, all my mates were at it, but when I looked at my Nana I thought, 'Fuck me, I do not want to end up like that'. So I've never smoked. She lived a full life, had a family and had achieved what she wanted to. I just wish she was still around now to see me doing all the things I used to tell her I dreamed of achieving. She was my number one fan.

I've shed a tear for all the friends I've lost to racing, but maybe I haven't properly grieved for them yet. To be honest, I'm not entirely sure I know exactly what grieving is. I've heard priests telling us to celebrate the life of someone we've lost, so I try to do that. You can look at all the pictures and remember all the good times, but life is short and you only get one go. As selfish as that sounds, that's where I am on death.

*

My first podium for Birdy was at Cadwell in 1996 in the rain. There used to be two 250 races back then so you had a couple of shots at it. There was also prize money. You might win £300 for coming eighth, £500 for a fifth. Racing was just about wiping its gob for me with the prize money topping up the work I was doing for Birdy. I was running the truck (on red diesel, obviously) and things were just about working. I was living in Becky's mum and dad's house and when we weren't there we were off racing, camping in the truck. I was gradually carving my way in to the race paddock. Picking up a bit of a name for myself, popping up on the radar now and then.

He would never tell me back then and he obviously couldn't tell me now, but I think there was a little spark between me and Joey back then in 1996. I raced at Scarborough that year and road racing was still fairly new to me. I just wanted to do as many races as I could. I got a free entry and Paul Bird had chipped in a bit of money. Off we went.

I was learning my way round and going OK, running near the front with Alan Patterson, Joey and a few of the top riders. In the second to last race I burnt my clutch out. Obviously I had no spares, so I was stuffed. In the meantime, Joey had finished the race and couldn't be bothered to do the last one. He went straight into the Irish Embassy (as his Dunlop race tent was called) and was on the vodka with all the Paddies. After a drink, he went out and did a parade lap on a classic bike, rode back into the paddock and backed it into the tent, which was still packed full of people. He was revving the nuts out of the thing while everyone was laughing and joking. I was on the scrounge for parts and asked him if he had any clutch plates for my 250. He went straight to his bike, laid it over on its side and took the clutch pack straight out there and then. He handed it to me and I put it in my bike. I finished third in the last race of day then took it out and gave it back to him.

He didn't need to do that. He knew who I was by then, but I wasn't really on his radar. I'd had a bit of a ride with him at the North West previously, then I'd taken his bike to the TT and I was going okay in the British Championship, so yeah, he'd have known who I was. But I wouldn't have thought he was bothered about anyone else out on track, let alone me. He just always seemed to be so focused on doing his own thing.

Despite how cocky I was everywhere else when I was growing up, I was never a smart arse in the race paddock. When I look at people in the paddock now, a lot of them seemed to be gobshites. When they come and ask for stuff, I don't feel like giving them anything. Not all of them of course. If Lee Johnston asked me to lend him something I'd do it straight away. He's cheeky, he's funny and he's carving his career. There are no edges to him and I like that. Other people I find it difficult to deal with. Joey must have been in that same boat as me now back when I was asking him for parts.

*

In 1997 Birdy got us an Aprilia 250. Brains came on board as our fulltime mechanic and Birdy ran the team. Steve Patrickson rode the 125 Honda and I was on the Aprilia. Again, Birdy said he wanted me to try and find some money for the team. I said I'd have to work it off for him. I did just that, driving about delivering stuff, doing whatever needed to be done for him.

That year we did the lot, British championship, Scarborough, North West, TT. I went to Daytona and raced out there. Birdy sent us off on this adventure. Me, Brains and my best mate Glyn. We carried bits of bike with us on the plane to make sure we had them when we needed them and creased up laughing as we loaded cylinder heads onto the X-ray machine at the airport. We hired a car in the States and stayed in motels on the way to Daytona. We did a club race there to get our eye in before the AMA race. Even if you were a racer, they used to kick you out of the circuit at 6pm there so there was nowhere to work on the bike. So every night we took it home with us, stuck it in the lift and kept it in our motel room. It was mega.

By now I was starting to win the odd race and grab a pole position here and there. I made my first TT podium in '97 on a 250 Aprilia. I also raced on a 125 Aprilia that broke down in every practice session. In the race it flew! We used to get up in the freezing cold at five in the morning to go out for morning practice. I'd be there in my leathers and a hoody, jumping from foot to foot to try and keep warm. Ten minutes later the little thing would be seized up and leant against a wall. I'd be swearing at it, banging my boots on the floor to warm up and warming my hands under my armpits while I waited for a lift back to the pits.

We were sick of the little thing by the time it came to the last practice session, so the boys put a knackered piston in it. They'd rubbed it down so there was loads of clearance, banking on it blowing up as soon as possible. At the end of my first lap, the team were having cups of tea thinking I'd pull into the pits. I screamed past them; the bike was running perfectly.

I remember Birdy had one of those poncey fold-out mobile phones that cost a fortune in the late nineties. He gave it to me and told me to call him when the bike had broken down. Somehow I managed to lose the thing instantly and he ended up spewing. Anyway, during the race I was in the top five or six, going well, when the bloody bike started misfiring. I stopped and took my helmet off for a closer look, swearing at the thing the whole time. It had power valves that opened and closed if they were hooked up to a battery pack. The terminals were hanging off so I grabbed a penny from a marshal and switched the spare battery pack in. We'd planned to change it over in the pit stop and we used to keep the spare one under the seat. I lobbed the old battery in the hedge, stuck my helmet back on and got going again. I finished the ultra-lightweight race in 12th place, bagging a bronze replica.

The main event for me, though, was the lightweight 250 race. I didn't know that I'd end up riding for Honda the following year, but they must have been watching my TT career. If they weren't, I soon put myself on their radar because in 1997 I started the lightweight race in 26th place and finished in third, bagging the fastest lap of the race on the last lap. I was motoring. Even though I still felt like I was learning my way around the place, that Aprilia was probably the quickest bike on the track. When it hit the note, it was a jet. I was rocking past people while I was learning and posted a faster lap each time. I didn't even realise I was doing it because I had no pit boards or anything. When I crossed the line, everyone was peaking. A lad called Gary Dynes had dropped out of the race from third with a gearbox problem, handing me the last step on the podium behind Ian Lougher and Joey Dunlop. In two attempts at the TT I'd gone from 15th place to standing on the podium next to the greatest road racer that ever lived, with a 116.8mph fastest lap under my belt. I felt absolutely honoured to be in Joey's presence up there. The same guy I'd idolised for all those years, the same man whose name I'd cut out and stuck to my bedroom wall. Still winning and still way cooler than he realised.

I did the fastest lap of the race that day on the 250 but Joey had done the damage at the start of the race and blitzed us all. He did his job without ever showing much emotion. He'd come up the return road after a race and everyone would be clapping and cheering him, but he'd barely lift a hand from the bars to wave, riding straight past everybody on his way into the winner's enclosure. To me he was a god. I used to wonder if he was feeling anything after those wins, but I suppose he just enjoyed being on the bike, spinning his own spanners and riding his own race.

To say it was a special moment for me is a bit of an understatement. It was the greatest moment of my career up to that point. Gary Dynes, the lad who dropped out of third that day, isn't with us anymore, and his name is another that people seem to have forgotten.

*

That same year I made my four-stroke debut at the TT. It was down to John Clucas who was on the spanners on the 250 I rode for Birdy. John's dad offered to build me a brand new Honda 600. It was a nice bike with some good kit on it, but I couldn't get it to go in a straight line. I felt sorry for the guy who owned it. John Clucas senior was one of the nicest blokes you could ever meet and I was shit on his bike. I couldn't understand the thing, it felt too big and gave me no confidence. Other two-stroke riders made the change easily but I jumped on and hated it.

The one thing I regret more than anything else in my career is staying on the smaller-capacity bikes for too long. When I eventually won the British 250cc Championship in 1999, that should have been my time to move on to big bikes and not look back. I had a bit of a mental block with them though. I just couldn't get on with them to begin with. Becky still reminds me about the first time I got off the 600 Honda and threw a wobbler. Apparently I tried to kick the telly in, shouting 'I'm not riding one of them fucking diesels, they're not proper racing bikes, they're a pile of shit!'. I can't remember that, but I do know that I just didn't click with them.

John Clucas senior put a load of money into that 600 for me to ride, but I loathed it. It threw a rod going into Ballacraine in practice and I had to borrow an engine from Joey. I finished the Junior TT in 24th place, getting beaten by Sandra Barnett. It's the only race I've ever finished at the TT without winning a replica. I think that result wounded me and held my career up as far as four-strokes were concerned. Again, Becky tells me that I came in from the race, jumped off and told her that it was a piece of diesel shit.

I look at how guys like DJ, Chris Walker and Michael Rutter went straight onto the big bikes and stuck with them until they'd got their heads around how to ride them, and I wish I'd done the same. I had nobody pushing me to do that though. By this stage of my racing career, my dad had realised that he couldn't have as much input into my decisions as he used to have so he kind of left me to it. It was just me and Becky talking to each other about this stuff, when maybe I should have had a manager at the table telling me what was going to be what. I should have moved up and I didn't. I guess it was because I was flying on the two-strokes. I just got too comfortable on them and decided to stick with what I knew. I think that's held me back a bit, despite the success I've had. It definitely helped me miss my chance in BSB.

To be honest, I was so wrapped up in the Paul Bird two-stroke thing that I wasn't looking far enough down the line to think about my long-term career. What me and him did together was great, it came along at exactly the right time and he's always looked after me, but back then he kind of owned me and I was too young and wet behind the ears to know any different. I chose the easier route, stuck with what I knew and everyone seemed happy. I know I was. Some people have their own reasons for not always liking Paul and we've had our ups and downs but he backed me from the start and I'll always be grateful for that.

Away from that miserable 600 ride, 1997 was a year that I was living the dream. It might sound cocky, but I don't think I realised how good I was in '96. I started to get my head around that in 1997. I won my first British Championship race, at Knockhill, where I qualified on pole, had five podiums in the Championship and finished the season in fifth. I got the 250 wildcard for the British Grand Prix at Donington, finishing 14th and in the points. I won at Scarborough, got on the podium at the North West and finished fifth at Daytona. Things were going really well on that Aprilia.

*

In 1998 it was Honda's 50th anniversary, so they made a massive effort. They had the factory RVFs there, plus Simmo, Phil McCallen and what felt like endless amounts of money to put into everything. Honda really wanted to win the 250 race and they couldn't rule out me stopping that from happening because I'd posted the fastest lap the year before. At the time, I was still naïve and a bit green. Honda wanted me on one of their bikes, so Birdy dealt with Honda. I still don't know what he got paid for running the bike and me but I didn't really care. I just wanted to race.

I remember bumping in to Charlie Williams in the TT paddock very early in my road riding career and he told me that one day I'd have a Honda contract under my arm. Charlie was a seven times TT winner, a lot older than me and a racer I really looked up to. He was the main man on a 350 in the late 1970s and early eighties and was a lap record holder. I couldn't believe what Charlie was saying to me. A factory Honda contract and me, I don't think so! But there I was, a couple of years later with a Honda deal on my plate.

Thanks to Honda, I was on a Vimto-sponsored RS250 with a trick TSR chassis. On top of that, I got to ride a 500 in the North West and the TT, and was the wildcard in the British 500cc Grand Prix. There was all sorts going on.

So yeah, 1998 was a good year. I wasn't making any wages as such, but the racing was wiping its mouth. I finished third in the TT in the wet behind Joey on a Honda and Bob Jackson on a Yamaha. I also finished fourth in the British 250 Championship for Birdy. I bagged a fifth in the 250 race at the North West, as well as a fourth and a fifth in the big bike races on the 500. Getting the chance to race with Doohan, Biaggi, Barros and Simon Crafar (who won), in the 500GP at Donington was special. I finished the race in the points in 12th place, ahead of Garry McCoy and a couple of other guys. Scott Smart was the only other British rider on the grid that day. He finished tenth.

CHAPTER 10

Disneyland for Adults

LATER THAT YEAR I had my first Macau experience. Now I had three TTs, four North West 200s and some road racing at Scarborough under my belt, it sort of fell into my lap. It was one of those events which starts off as just conversation. I'd heard about it, what it was like to ride and the craic that you have while you're there. The fact it was called a Grand Prix seemed to get people excited. It sounds the bollocks telling your mates you've entered a GP on the other side of the world.

There was no such thing as YouTube back then so I didn't know much about what it was like to actually ride at Macau, but that didn't stop me having a nibble at Paul Bird to see if he fancied entering it. Birdy wasn't that keen, so I asked him if he'd mind me trying to get a ride with Joe Millar. I was keen to tick Macau off the list because Portugal was handing control of Macau back to China in 1998 and everyone thought that the Chinese wouldn't let the racing continue.

Joe ran a team at Macau every year. He was a businessman from Northern Ireland who loved racing. In the 1980s, he sponsored a TT winner called Eddie Laycock, who beat Hizzy in the 250 race in 1987 and won a 400cc TT in 1989. Joe Millar also backed Jeremy McWilliams, Michael Rutter, Eugene McManus and a couple of other guys at international level. He'd been running 500cc bikes in Grand Prix for years. He had a 500cc V-twin NSR that Scott Smart had been riding in GPs. So I spoke to Joe about riding it at Macau and he said yes straight away. Boom, job done. Brains would be on the spanners and I thought we'd be away. I didn't have a clue, but packed my leathers, helmet and a few T-shirts into a suitcase and jumped on a plane.

I'd flown to Spain, Daytona and a few other bits and pieces, but I'd never done proper long haul before. I landed in Hong Kong and got straight on the boat to Macau. It was weird from the off. I expected it to be hot but I didn't realise what humidity was until I stepped off that plane. The food was weird and the culture was very different to what I was used to. I loved it. Casinos, bright lights, prostitutes and lady boys everywhere, it was all new for me and Brains and it was a real eye opener. We went straight to an Irish bar and I got pissed out of my head, spewing my ring up everywhere with the drink and the jetlag. It was messy from the word go.

All the boys were there, DJ, Ronnie Smith and Michael Rutter, and we had a proper good time. As long as your wallet is fat enough, you can do whatever you want. You can be a full factory tourist if you like, head to Taipei and see the sights, or just go on the piss and see the weird side of Macau. I've never really been interested in the darker side of it all and some the lads take the piss, but it doesn't really do anything for me.

I've seen people go out there and fall in love with a Russian and end up married. You can find love in Macau, you can also find snide Rolex watches and get caught out by lady boys. It's a 24-hour-a-day, seven-day-a-week, neon-lit gambling-based Disneyland for adults, with dangerous motorbike racing thrown into the mix for good measure. Like Las Vegas, it's fucked up and demented, but it sounds good on paper so you go.

That first year I went out there, Jenson Button came and sat on my bike. He was racing in Formula Three or 3 and was just mooching about the place. I've seen Lewis Hamilton, Rosberg, Vettel and all the big names in F1 come through Macau and go on to become racing gods. Macau is more important to those boys than it is to bike racers. I've also seen loads of deals being closed in Macau. Pissed-up clever talk in the bar can turn into serious sponsorship deals that have launched entire careers.

I qualified in the top ten, but wasn't at the sharp end. I got a decent start and was hanging in there, but Rutter and Simmo were gone. Riding at Macau is nothing like riding at the TT. The concentration required for Macau is intense because it's massively technical. There are lots of corners on top of each other and it's a constant physical effort. It also all looks the same. There are no trees or particular kerbs to pick as braking markers, just a barrier running pretty much all the way round the place. You end up getting tunnel vision. You ride fast at Macau just by using feel and engine rpm.

At the TT, you go down the Sulby Straight and you can suck on a few breaths and shake your arms and legs off if you need to. Macau isn't like that. It's much more like a short circuit, with zero run off. Granted you can't make a mistake at the TT, but you can run wide here and there if you overcook it. You definitely can't make a mistake at Macau. If you do, you're going straight into a barrier.

That said, you can clip a barrier at Macau and not come off. Everyone's done that. You can pinball off and keep going fine. All you'll pick up is a few scuffs on your leathers. I've hit them hard and carried on. In 2016 Conor Cummins put a dent in his helmet hitting the barrier and still finished the race.

Having said that, it's mad, when you think about it, hanging a big fast bike out on a street circuit in China. Let's be honest, if you get it wrong you'll probably be having a bowl of soup and a glass of water for Christmas dinner that year as the race is usually held at the end of November. When the plane takes off on the Monday after the races, if you've had a proper spill the boys will wave you goodbye as they bugger off home. Nobody is going to stay behind to tuck you in at night.

As much as I say I wouldn't want to be stuck there blending my Christmas dinner in a hospital, the place is like a magnet and it draws you back in year after year. The lads that do race out there end up having a twisted mess of a craic together. We all go on the piss for a few days, without really shaking off the jetlag, and end up in a bit of a daze, right up to the point where you let the clutch out and fire the bike down the road. That wakes you up.

That first year, there was another rider, a German fella called Gerhard Lindner. His bike was as trick as fuck. He was fast and about ten seconds ahead of me in third. I was in no man's land, about ten seconds ahead of the guy behind me. I was ticking the laps down, concentrating hard but soaking in the atmosphere and enjoying myself. On the last lap I came banging down the gears going into the hairpin and the German was on his arse on the track. I could see he was okay and just thought, 'You beauty!'. All I had to do was get round the last corner and I'd be on the podium.

So yeah, I had a fairy-tale start to my Macau racing career. Finishing third in my race was special but you could tell we weren't expecting much because I stood on the podium wearing Vimto leathers and I'd ridden a Millar bike. I went out for that race in '98 thinking it'd be the last one ever and 19 years later it's still going strong.

*

In 1999 I won the 250 British Championship, making the podium 12 times, with five pole positions and two race wins. That championship win was massive to me. I'd worked like a dog in the 250 series for years to get to that point. Even now people assume that I've only ever been a road racing specialist. It kind of pisses me off. I beat some quality guys to win that championship and rode really well all year. I finished second at Daytona, won at Scarborough and at the Stars of Darley. At the TT, I did the business in the 250 race and won it. Fifteenth in '96, third in '97 and '98 and then a win in '99. Four laps, 150.92 miles and I crossed the line 33 seconds ahead of Jason Griffiths in second place and Gavin Lee in third. That year I'd made the decision to push as hard as I could on the first lap, to try and put as big a dent as possible into the other riders. It worked.

Did I want to beat Joey when we were in the same race? Of course I did. He set off number three and I started number four, I wanted to beat him as much as I wanted to beat everyone else out there. I also broke Ian Lougher's long-standing lap record while I was at it. Obviously I wanted to win, but I didn't feel like I'd pushed myself out of my comfort zone safety-wise. I rode within my limits, the bike worked really well because I had a good team around me and I did the job for all of us. It also felt good to chalk up my first TT victory in the same year that Dave Jefferies had his first win in the Formula One race on his V&M R1. I've still got the bottle of Champagne from the podium celebrations that day. Little keepsakes like that mean a lot to me.

So suddenly I've got a free ride and I'm actually making a few quid. Things were starting to come together. People had stopped asking me to dip my hand in my pocket. It felt great finally being able to buy a round of drinks, or to take Becky out for a meal if we fancied it.

Stuart Bland was another full-time mechanic for Birdy by then. I got him the job. Blandy had previously worked at a local plant-hire firm called Hartley Hire. The year before he'd been with the team part time and then came in full time for '99. Thanks to Birdy, I always had the best tackle. Kit-part 250s, full time mechanics, trick Aprilias. I delivered, he delivered and we both scratched each other's backs. But I was getting interest – a few new doors that were opening – and it started to feel like it was time to move on. I didn't act on it though, or go looking for a ride with a new team. Maybe I was just comfortable being comfortable again. If I'd had a personal manager, things might have been different.

CHAPTER 11

Joey

IN 2000 I was blessed with the opportunity to ride as teammate to Joey Dunlop. I also made the change up to big four-stroke bikes, riding an SP1 Honda. Joey accepted me, we were friends despite me still being in awe every time I saw the guy. He allowed me into his house, and into his garage too. Nobody got to go in there. There were bits of bike everywhere, stuff on the walls and piles of leathers in the corner. When I looked through them, Rothmans, V&M and others, they all told a story to me. I keep my leathers lined up on hangers. Joey's were just stacked on top of each other. There were helmets literally rolling round on the floor. Beauties sponsored by Downtown Radio just kicking about the place.

When you consider that as a teenager I'd had the letters of his name stuck to my bedroom wall with all the pictures I could find of him, I was like a kid in a sweetshop. I'd pick up old fairings and tell him the story of the race that they were from. He allowed me into his life and I'll never forget how good that made me feel.

People mention me in the same breath as Joey in terms of the number of wins we've had over at the TT, and they're right to do so because I've earned every one of them. But, Joey was so much more than a TT racer. He was also five times Formula One world champion. He'd win the Ulster Grand Prix, then the TT, then he'd pack up and drive to Portugal and win out there. From there he'd drive up to Assen and do the same. People forget that in the first ever round of the World Superbike Championship, Joey stood on the podium with Davide Tardozzi and Marco Lucchinelli. I could never achieve that. I'm fast round the Isle of Man but I couldn't jump off my superbike straight onto a 125 and go and win. The thing would disappear up my arse crack. It was a different era, a different time.

So in 2000, I was in his garage watching him staring at carb jets with a pair of glasses, peering down his nose at them. To me he looked like an old teacher or old scientist. He didn't look like a 125 winner who could switch on the magic when he got on a bike. It was unreal. I was looking at his trophy collection and he had stuff from races in Europe that none of us had ever heard of. Hand-carved wooden bears for winning races in Estonia and suchlike.

You get a feel for the kind of man he was from what he did when he saw footage of orphaned Romanian children on the telly. He filled his truck with clothes and food, and welded the back doors shut to stop people from robbing him on the way. Then he set off. He slept in the cab on the journey, roughing it. When he got there, he ground the weld off the back of the truck and gave every last thing he had to those poor kids. He wasn't just a bike racer, he was a man of his word and he fully deserved the OBE that he was awarded in recognition for helping others.

I watched him stick his Honda SP1 on pole at the North West 200 when he was 48. A kit SP1 was a pretty good bike, but it wasn't like an R7/1 or anything. I couldn't believe it. I hated the SP1 and was all over the road on the fucking thing. As with John Clucas senior's CBR600 I genuinely couldn't keep it going in a straight line. I asked him how he'd managed it and he said, 'Ah just fockin' grit yer teeth.' Grit your teeth?!

I had some fearsome stability issues with the Vimto SP1 at the North West and had taken it back to Joey's house to work on it before the race. We tried to get access to a local airfield to test after we'd made some changes but couldn't get on. Joey said he'd ride it up the road to check it was okay. He set off and was soon out of sight, I could hear him feeding the bike gears, hard on the gas. He lived on a long straight road and was pretty much flat out on the thing before long.

I had a brew on the go and was just hanging around in the garage when the police turned up at the house. I didn't know what to do and was shitting myself. Joey was long gone. The first copper climbed out of the car and said, 'All right lads?' We all nodded and said hello while we looked at the floor, kicking stones, trying to play it cool. The second copper then piped up, 'Ah, Joey just passed us there, he must have been doing 150mph!' We were caught red-handed.

Then the second copper simply said, 'There was no way we were going to catch him, but when you see him would you wish him all the best for the race on Saturday from us?' That's the level of affection Joey had in his hometown. We didn't know, but Joey had shat himself when he saw the police car and was hiding in his mate's garden a few miles up the road. He rang the phone at the house and asked us to come and pick him up.

*

I arrived on the Isle of Man feeling like I was Jack the lad when it came to the 250 TT race. I thought, 'I'm going to beat Joey, I'll have him in this race. I'll catch him up and get past and that'll be it, job done'. I was leading the 250 British championships on the mainland and I was the new lap record holder at the TT; I was rubbing my hands together at the prospect of a win. When the race started I didn't even see which way he went. He absolutely smoked me and I couldn't believe it. I was wounded. I got the tiniest glimpse of him once coming out of Union Mills, then I never saw him again.

I still think about that race a lot now. The only way I can get my head around how quick Joey was that day was because of an aggressive pass I put on him during practice. It was along Glentramman and I roughed him up a little bit as I went by. It was a harsh pass and you should never ever do that to anybody at that place. I felt sick when I did it, it's not in my nature to be like that. I just came up on him and thought, 'There's Joey, he's having this'. He never showed his cards early in the week during practice, when I was going faster than anyone else like a twat. I knew that move was going to come back on me and it did. He annihilated me in that race. When I'm passing people at the TT now, it's with a bit of respect and it all goes back to that pass I put on Joey.

Anyway, the move wound him up, I know it did. He must have decided there and then that he was going to beat me in the race. Afterwards he wasn't smug, but when he was interviewed, he said something like 'Well that showed him', and threw me a wink. I had masses of respect for Joey anyway, but after that race it went up.

It was a year of highs on track, as well as some crushing blows both on and off it. I won at Daytona and at the North West on the 250, had a TT win on the single cylinder Chrysalis bike and managed to get third in the

Formula One race, finishing behind Michael Rutter in second and Joey who won it. It was my first podium in the Superbike race and it felt like another chance for my and Joey's paths to cross. Call it destiny, I just thought it was cool to be near enough to him to spray Champagne on him on his 24th TT win. I was living the dream. I reminded him of the day back in 1986 when I asked him to sign a picture of himself and told him that we'd be teammates but he couldn't remember it. He just give me a smile like he used to and said, 'Yeah, yeah son.' I didn't mind a bit. It would have taken a fair whack to knock the shine off that day for me.

At the NW200 that year he was black-flagged and he went fucking mad. He was running in third place and his back tyre started coming apart, there were bits of it flying everywhere. 'I've never been fucking black flagged in my life, what are you doing?' he shouted at the race organisers. He stamped his feet with them and then his team, telling them that the bike wasn't good enough and it needed more of everything. He got it as well, a factory bike with an Aaron Slight engine, fancy back end and proper electronics. They gave it to him in time for the TT and he delivered. He won the Superbike race when nobody thought he could do it. It was unreal.

The thing that changed everything for me in that race in 2000 was swapping from Dunlop to Pirelli tyres at the very last minute. I went from nowhere in practice week to standing on the podium in the race. Same bike, same settings, just different tyres. The bike felt like it was trying to bounce off the kerbs in straight lines until we swapped the tyres over. Nowadays Dunlop are totally dominant but back then it was all about Pirellis. But Joey stuck with the Dunlops and still won the race, which had me scratching my head about his talent even more. I wondered how much quicker he might have been if he'd gone for the Pirellis like me.

*

Around this time my friendship with Jim Moodie developed. Moodie can be a difficult bloke. If he likes you, you have half a chance of him talking to you. If he doesn't like you, he'll just fuck you off out of it. I forced myself onto him when he was winning TT races. I wanted to be mates with anyone that was winning. Ian Lougher, Brian Reid, Hizzy and all the other winners, I used to hang around them until they'd talk to me. I remember buying an Arai helmet from Jim once at the side of the motorway. I met him in his big camper, gave him the cash and he was off. It was a way to get to meet him and talk to him.

I could bump into Steve Hislop and lose an hour to him while he went into detail about a certain section of the course. Later on, he'd tell me about the '91 Senior race and how he closed Joey down on the roads, doing all the movements of the bike with his hands as he talked. Hizzy was happy to share everything and was brilliant company.

They were all great company, apart from Carl Fogarty. Foggy is either shy or arrogant or a bit of the two mixed together. He was hard to get to know. He was always too busy for me. I met him on the ferry once when I was nothing more than a fan and he was more interested in Becky. You can't take his determination away from him though. He was hard charging and won TTs and World Championships. I have massive respect for him as a rider, but I don't know the real man.

He also owes me 30 quid and that hurts. We were all out for dinner in London a few years ago, Whitham, Hutchy, Foggy and me, and he just thought that he didn't need to pay. I went to the toilet and when I came back he'd gone without chipping in. Hutchy and Whitham are from Yorkshire so there was no chance of them paying and I had to pick up the bill for him! He's probably got more money than the three of us put together and should have toed the line. Where I come from he'd have got filled in for that. His battle with Hizzy round the Isle of Man has been voted as one of the greatest races ever. I can't take that away from him and wouldn't want to, but in my book he should have paid his way and didn't.

I thought Hizzy was a better rider on the roads than Carl. He was magic to watch and really raised the bar at the TT. He was doing 124mph laps in practice in 1991 and the track wasn't anywhere near as quick as it is now. And he was doing it on a 750. It might have been a factory 750, but it wasn't a 1000. That means going down the big straights at 170 mph rather than the 200 we can manage on the big bikes. It was a hell of an achievement. So smooth, fast and stylish.

Anyway, when I first saw Jim Moodie and his bloody great big American motorhome I thought, 'He's doing something right and I want to know him'. Jim being Jim, he wouldn't let you into his business if he didn't think you were all right. He was clever and thorough and did his deals right. He was successful on and off track. He was also unbelievably hard and stuck to his morals. I respected him for that. He won eight TTs but because he's no longer in the limelight people seem to have forgotten that. He's still fiercely competitive, does a lot of cycling and sends me pictures of how many miles he's pedalled up however many hills. None of it makes any sense to me but what is clear is that he still has that passion to win and that killer instinct in him. I think that's why he stays away from the racing scene now.

In a way, Jim gave me a chance back in 2000 when he fell out with Honda. He didn't want to ride the new Fireblade. He thought it was uncompetitive and said so. He stuck to what he believed and Honda sacked him for it. He was the lap record holder the year before on an RC45. He broke Foggy's longstanding record from a standing start and then the tyre delaminated on the second lap of the race. The pace he showed on the RC45 in '99 meant he had a Honda deal for 2000. He was riding the Castrol bike in the British championship and had a TT ride all sorted. He won the 600 race but wouldn't ride the new Blade in the Senior after experiencing it in practice.

When Honda sacked him, Jim fought them and took them to court. He asked me to be a witness, so I agreed. Jim lost the case but went on to win the British championship that year, finishing on a Yamaha R6. Standing in court for him was the right thing to do and afterwards he said he owed me one. I was mates with him by then, but I thought it was good to have a favour from him tucked in my pocket for a rainy day.

When Honda let Jim go, I got his Castrol Honda 600 ride in the British Championship, plus my 250 in British as well. So the year was going great for me. I had two competitive bikes, was leading the British 250 Championship and was going okay on the 600. I'd had a podium at the TT on the Superbike and everything was looking good.

*

On Sunday, 2 July 2000, I'd just won a 250 British Championship race at Silverstone and was walking through the paddock feeling good about myself when I heard that Joey had been killed. I thought it was a joke. Race bike builder and mechanic Mark Hanna told me but I shrugged it off like he was taking the piss. I was in a state of utter disbelief. You think you and all your pals are invincible and that these things don't happen to people like you, until they do. Split second, blink of an eye and they're gone.

Part of me wished that if he had to be killed on a bike, it should have been on a glorious sunny day at a packed Ulster Grand Prix, not tucked away at a nothing race in Estonia on a 125. It felt like the penalty didn't fit the crime. It's because of horrible situations like that that I question what I'm doing when I go out in a wet race. I'd hate to end up stuck in a wheelchair thinking, 'Why the fuck did I do that?' I'd be so angry with myself for risking it all when I didn't need to.

The reason Joey was at that race was because his good friend and long-time sponsor Andy McMenemy had committed suicide about a month or so before. Joey wanted to get away for a bit on his own to get his head around what had happened. I guess fate isn't something you can control.

Honda had previously given Joey his RC45 race bike, which was chained to the ceiling in the bar he owned. He unbolted it and lifted it from the wall, loaded it, a 600 and a 125 into his van and set off on his own to go and road race on a tiny 3.7 mile circuit in Estonia. He won the wet 600 race on the Saturday and the wet superbike race on the RC45. It started raining again during the 125 race and three laps in he crashed and was killed.

There are a lot of ways to look at how things played out for Joey. I see it like this: you can play Russian roulette for 20 years, but eventually you're going to get one in the head. I don't want to sound disrespectful, but there has to come a time when you stop doing what we do and Joey wasn't ever going to stop. We'll never truly understand the pain of those that have lost sons, dads and brothers but if my dad had raised me well and I'd watched him as my hero win 26 TTs, only to lose him when he was 48 years old, fuck me I'd take the positives out of that. I'd think about what a great guy he was. I wouldn't let anybody come and tell me that my dad was an arsehole.

I think about the amazing career Joey had. He had the pub and there was a legacy for his family. You hear stories all the time of pisshead dads who roll in at two in the morning and knock their wives about. They live to 70 and achieve fuck all, leaving nothing behind but aggro and a trail of shit. Joey Dunlop was not one of those men.

*

Joey said his last words to me at the end of a civic reception they held for him in mid-June in his hometown of Ballymoney. He stood on the top of an open-top bus and waved to his fans. Me, Bob McMillan and Roger Harvey turned up without him knowing to support him. He was really happy to see us. I wanted to be there and I didn't need any excuse to go and have a beer with him. When we were up there on the bus he leaned in and said that he wasn't happy with all the attention and just wanted to get back to his bar for a few beers. After he'd been given the freedom of the town and the ceremony was finished, we went straight back to the pub.

That night was special. We got absolutely fucking banjoed. He wouldn't let me buy a single drink and when he eventually gave in and let me buy him one, he served me and gave me a Manx ten-pound note as change. Stitched me up. I've still got it at home. Like most men in any part of Ireland, Joey loved a drink. The number of people I still meet who claim to have had a beer with him is hilarious. It's like every man in Ireland has been on the drink with him.

God knows what time it was when we finished drinking, but Joey drove us back to the guesthouse we were staying at a few miles down the road in his Ford Mondeo. I was in the front, feeling like a king because I was sitting next to Joey Dunlop. He looked at me and said, 'Thanks for coming, it means a lot'. I said goodbye, jumped out and slammed the door. That was the last time I ever saw him. After I'd followed him for years and years, those were big words to me. As people who knew Joey well would tell you, he didn't say a lot about anything and you would never be accepted into his clan if he didn't like you. It was as simple as that and I felt like I was in his clan. He'd taken me into his home and his garage, and had shown me everything that made him who he was. Knowing Joey like that was magical for me.

My very last memory of him was him driving the Ford Mondeo across the front garden of the boarding house and straight over the rockery. He wrecked the lot. The owner came out and was screaming, 'What the fuck?' at us. Then he clocked who was driving and just said, 'Is that Joey?' When I said it was, his face lit up into a smile. Then he laughed and left us to it.

I wanted to go to the funeral but I got a wildcard to race at Donington in the 500cc Grand Prix. Valentino Rossi won the race from Kenny Roberts Jr and Jeremy McWilliams. I finished in 13th place after qualifying in 18th. Meanwhile, 50,000 people had turned out for Joey's funeral. The man was a god, he was worshipped wherever he went and had been a lifelong idol for me. He was my hero, my teammate and my friend, yet I missed the funeral to go and race motorbikes. If you're wondering how strong the pull of the sport can be, me missing that funeral to race in the GP at Donny speaks volumes.

Guys like Joey lived and breathed racing. They grew up around bikes and lived with the knowledge that they hurt you. Nobody wants to see anybody die and I tried to look for the positives rather than dwelling on his death. Imagine the sights that man saw. All those times he walked to the top step on the podium, all those race wins, what a life to have lived. And even after all that success, he wasn't a strutter. He had no idea how massively popular he was. Completely unassuming. I always wondered why when he won a TT he'd never acknowledge a clap or a high five on the return road. He just rode past everyone while they were yipping and cheering for him. It's like they weren't even there to him. It used to make me wonder how he got his kicks from racing. I suppose if we were all the same the world would be a boring place. A man who is happy to pull a factory Honda 250 out of the back of the van, wheel it through a load of mud and then lean it up against the shed to do the clutch is just different from everyone else. Joey Dunlop was definitely different. He was a hero from the day I saw him lean his race bike against the paper shop window and nip in for fags until the day he died. He still is now. But like I said when my Nana died, I'm not one to hang around and dwell on death. I've cried for Joey in the past and I'm sure I will again, but life has to keep moving.

CHAPTER 12

Shit Sandwich

BACK IN THE team, things weren't quite right between me and Paul Bird. We weren't getting on because Paul and Becky weren't. Paul called the shots and said that he didn't want Becky to come racing with me. It was just the way Paul operated, he had his own ways. He banned Stuart Easton's wife Claire from going racing with him a few years back. She ignored him and it rocked the boat.

Despite Paul telling Becky not to be there, she turned up to a race meeting and it had pissed him off. He's a boss and they do what they have to do to get the best out of people. I can respect him for that now and we get on well. But when I crashed at Oulton Park on my 250 in 2000 things came to a head. I called him from a phonebox to tell him I'd broken my leg following a crash on the out-lap. I said it was going to be three months before I was ready to ride again. Paul said not to worry about it because I was up the road anyway. He fired me there and then over the phone and sent me a letter to inform me that I was no longer employed by him. It's in a drawer in the house somewhere.

To be fair, Paul helped my career, but I think I helped him get to where he is now as well. I delivered him race wins, championship wins and TT wins, which help team owners as much as they help us riders. The irony is that I'd held on to two-strokes and ignored four-strokes for longer than I should have, but ten minutes before I broke my leg I'd dipped under the Oulton Park lap record on the Castrol Honda CBR600 that I'd replaced Jim Moodie on. The signs were all there, telling me I should be on the bigger bikes whether I liked them or not.

Thankfully I'd done enough that year in the time I'd spent on the 600 to bag the Castrol ride for 2001 in British Supersport. Plus I got on really well with the Castrol team manager, Roger Harvey. We clicked from the start. He was a former 125cc MX national champion and a good guy. Up until the point that there was a bone poking out of my leathers on the out lap on my 250, he liked what he saw.

Later that year I rode Paul's 500 at Macau. Becky went berserk but that was how me and Birdy worked together. I suppose I should have said no on moral grounds, but I didn't. Despite the way Paul handled me breaking my leg, I felt he'd looked after me in taking me on in the first place, plus when we worked well together we knew we were capable of getting good results.

When I say that 2000 was a year of ups and downs, I mean it. Becky and me broke up for a bit and we both did our separate thing. You can't have your cake and eat it. Those are the rules. Men get pissed off if someone else is shagging their woman but what's good for the goose is good for the gander. That's the situation we were in. When we got back together I ended up giving her a portion in a layby. Four pumps and a grunt later, the best thing in the world happened to us and our son Ewan was conceived.

*

I flew to Macau to race on Birdy's 500 with a leg that was still effectively broken. It meant a 12-and-a-half hour flight. I was in agony and shouldn't have been on the plane, never mind trying to race. I could barely walk. Dave Jefferies was waiting to meet me off the flight. He pushed me through the airport on top of a trolley full of suitcases. I was in tatters but I just wanted to ride. My leg and hip were in such rag order that I ended up wearing a Prexport boot on my right foot because I couldn't get my Daytona boot on. Up until then I was adamant about wearing Daytonas but I just couldn't ride with them on and had to borrow a pair of boots from Gus Scott. Rutter and DJ had a great duel for the win. Michael took it from David while I hobbled around on the 500 on agony.

After the race, we ended up going to Thailand for a few days on the piss. Those trips always got messy. Picture the scene, a handful of the handiest road racers on the planet, riding along on hired scooters wearing flip flops and shorts. Dave would spot an off-road section and we'd all have to stop for a ten-minute session of motocross at the side of the road. I ended up getting into a bit of a tussle with a German guy. Riding this scooter, I accidentally carved up this guy on a Harley Davidson. He chased us down the road to kick off with me and luckily Dave had my back. I've never been much of a fighter and didn't fancy rolling around on the floor with the bloke one bit.

Macau and Thailand afterwards was always a great laugh. One time the American team manager Henry De Grow had his missus out there with him. She had massive tits and Dave couldn't take his eyes off them. He wasn't interested in trying to sleep with her, he just had his radar permanently locked onto her breasts. I saw him leaving the hotel with her one day looking sheepish and asked him what he was up to. He told me that they were off on a cooking course together for the day. David Jefferies was no chef, but he sure did like looking at big tits, which is precisely what he did all day on that cooking course.

Dave was ace, he so was funny. He was a massive six-foot-two child. He drove refrigeration trucks in the winter for an extra few quid for the Manton group. He had a licence for everything and also did a bit in the family bike shop but I don't think he liked the idea of a proper job. He was always tinkering, making a car trailer or welding something together. He had toys everywhere; Range Rovers with massive wheels and tyres, and the Mitsubishi Shogun EVO that he used to fly about in. He even had a Russian armoured truck called a ZiL.

He was a mummy's boy. He lived in his garage, posters on the walls and trophies everywhere. When his tea was ready, his mum would ring a bell and he'd come through to the main part of the house to eat. He was also obsessed with porn. Me and him travelled the world together racing and everywhere we went, he either had a stash of porn DVDs with him or was looking to add to his collection. We became best friends through racing and I'd say it was down to the scrapes and adventures we'd end up getting into at the Macau GP.

*

I was quite shocked when Becky told me she was pregnant. I was young and my head was all over the place. We talked about it loads, looked at other people in paddocks that had managed to raise a family and realised it's just part of life. If anything, the prospect of having another mouth to feed drove me a bit harder to make sure I'd be able to cover the financial bases.

We were still living at Becky's mum and dad's in a single bed. And Becky wouldn't be working any time soon. We wanted a mortgage but couldn't get one because I didn't have proper books to present to the bank. It really wasn't great, especially when you consider that Becky was up the stick. We could have stayed and had the baby where we were – Becky's mum and dad were cool with it all – but we wanted our own space and it wouldn't have been fair on them.

And, to be honest, because I knew I was doing a season on the 600 Honda in British Supersport, I wanted to be Charlie Big Balls in the BSB paddock. That meant having a big 40-foot American coach. Jim Moodie sold me the one I wanted on a zero percent finance deal. It was a Fleetwood American Eagle. I think it was sixty grand and I only had half the money. We ended up living slightly out of our means to tell the truth.

But our options were to rent a flat, which felt like chucking money down the drain, or buy this motorhome off Jim Moodie and save like crazy for a year for the deposit we needed for a house. We went for it and basically lived like gypsies for over a year. We moved into the Fleetwood in February 2001, about two weeks before Becky was due to give birth with Ewan. It sounds crazy, looking back, but at the time it made sense and we were having fun.

*

I was in the room the day Ewan was born, with Becky's dad. I've seen a lot of things in my life but nothing prepares you for childbirth. That little furry triangle that you stick your fella in, to see a person come out of there like that is a phenomenon. A natural miracle that gave me a newfound respect for women. No epidural or drugs, Becky just dealt with the pain. It seems women expect to go through hell to have something that they will have lifelong affection for.

One of the first people I called with the news of Ewan's birth was David Jefferies. I said, 'Dave, I'm a dad!'. 'Right, I'll see you in a minute' he replied. He lived over in Yorkshire, miles away from us, but it was like he had a magic wand. He must have rallied his EVO flat out across the Yorkshire Dales because it felt like he was knocking in the door as soon as I put the phone down. We went out to wet the baby's head with a few of my close mates and got absolutely wankered. I've still got the bottle of Champagne that they all signed that night. It sits with the bottle I kept from standing on the podium with Joey.

I think the birth of my son brought me and Dave closer together. He was a softy at heart. He was a hard-charging man on a bike and he'd show anyone a wheel, but there was another side to him. He was affectionate and he got on really well with Becky. I'm not sure if it was just because of her tits, because he was obsessed with mammaries, but he would do anything for us and was a genuinely nice guy.

It's funny how you spend your whole life avoiding going anywhere near other people's shit, but when it's your baby, you have no problems getting on the end of a nappy with the stuff flying everywhere. It made me grow up.

We lived in the motorhome for about a year and a half before we saved enough money to move into the top half of the house that we own now. It was perfect for racing and we enjoyed living in it, but when I was away and Becky was stuck in it on her own with a new baby, I think she hated it. When I went off to Macau that year and decided to take in a few extra days with the lads in Thailand, I got David Jefferies to put the call in to Becky to tell her I wouldn't be home as early as I'd originally planned. She took the call from inside this freezing cold camper. DJ told Becky that I wasn't man enough to tell her myself. The motorhome had frozen over, so there was no hot water and baby Ewan was only about eight months old. It went down like a shit sandwich. Becky's dad went ballistic when he found out and moved her back home for a week or two to warm up. She told me she wasn't coming back. I thought the job was fucked.

I was riding the Castrol Honda CBR600 in the British Supersport championship, winning races and at the sharp end with Karl Harris and Kirk McCarthy. Everything was going well that year and I had good bikes lined up for the TT. I won at Macau as well, blitzed it in fact, which is why I ended up staying on for a few beers in Thailand with the lads, once DJ had put the call in to Becky. It felt things had started going my way.

Then there was the foot-and-mouth outbreak. That year's TT was cancelled and I was down a fair chunk of my salary. That meant we kind of did things on the cheap. We spent a month in Italy bouncing from cheap campsite to cheap campsite, or just parking up at the side of the road. We were hoping to have paid off the thirty grand we owed on it within a year. Jim's terms were simply to pay him back when I had the money. It felt a little bit like the wing and a prayer way I agreed to find the money that Birdy wanted when I first went racing for him. I knew I'd find a way somehow, but didn't quite know what it was. I shook on the deal and saved the worrying for another day.

*

Outside of winter, though, life in the motorhome was ace. When we'd finish a race weekend in the BSB paddock, we'd stay in it and get on the piss. Me, McCarthy, DJ, Glen Richards – maybe a dozen of us had nothing to get home for so we would get a camp fire going and have a few beers. DJ would pull up in some massive Volvo

Globetrotter truck with side exit exhausts and a body kit on it, pulling the air horns and flashing spotlights everywhere. He wasn't driving that thing to show off, he was just making himself happy in his own little world. He was making a few quid racing but him and his family worked bloody hard and they were entitled to it.

Ewan was just a baby so we didn't have to worry about school or anything and we enjoyed ourselves. We'd cruise back home to the campsite in Morecambe – Ocean Edge Caravan Park, just down the road from where we live now – when we were ready and park back up. There's nothing wrong with today's breed of racer, focusing on constantly training and maintaining what they think sponsors want to see. In their heads they're having a great time and I don't blame them for that. But there's something different about how they do things. Don't get me wrong, going on the piss and eating pie and chips clearly isn't the right way to go about being a racer. There is nothing wrong with being the ultimate, super-fit professional, but Dave and I seemed to be cut from different cloth and we didn't want to be in that world. We'd get to whatever paddock we were racing from, park next to each other and have a craic together. There's not many racers from back then still going now at 44 or 45 like I am. They've all grown up and moved on.

Honda has always given us a car to drive about in so we had that to make use of as well. We got a free pitch on the campsite, with free water and electricity, so we were basically able to tread water financially for the entire time we lived in it. There were shops and a swimming pool on site and we had a great time. People thought we were mental for doing it but me and Becky didn't. It was right for us at the time. Ewan was warm, fed, had clean clothes all the time and was loved. There's nothing wrong with the way you're living if you're doing right by your kids like that. It's not like we left him behind with a carer every time we went off racing. He came with us and we managed the work/home balance that people talk about. If anything, it helped draw us closer as a family. Obviously at times one of us would end up with cabin fever and get a bit short tempered but I've seen people do that in houses too.

I used to love it when Becky and Ewan would go to bed and I'd drive through the night. They'd wake up in the south of France or wherever and we'd have a bit of breakfast with the sun on our faces. We did stacks of miles, all the British rounds, holidays along the south coast, Scotland, the Swiss Alps and anywhere we fancied. We had no reason to come home, because wherever we parked up was home in that camper. And all the while people were asking us why we didn't have a mortgage and a nice flat somewhere in Morecambe. No thanks.

I was really proud of that motorhome and looked after it. There was always something going wrong with it that needed sorting but I didn't mind, that's what campers do. I really enjoyed the year, despite the lack of TT racing.

Then 2002 rolled up and I got offered the chance of racing in World Supersport on the Motorex Honda CBR 600. I thought this was my chance to go for everything I'd ever dreamed of. As well as the World SSP, it was a ticket to ride the North West and the TT, and all for more money than I'm earning now! It doesn't get much better than that, I thought. It meant that we'd be living in the camper for a bit longer than we'd planned, but it also meant that by the end of 2002 we'd be able to afford our first home.

I drove the Fleetwood all the way down to Valencia for a pre-season test. We had a week between testing and racing so we drove to Benidorm and shuffled about with all the old codgers. Nothing beats traveling round Europe in a massive motorhome with your whole family sat next to you. We travelled to hot countries for races and didn't bother coming back to the UK for weeks on end because the next race was also in Europe. There was no bad feeling about paying rent on a flat only to leave the thing empty most of the time while we swanned about the place.

Pick a European track and chances are we've lived in the car park. Big trips like leaving Monza after a world Supersport race on the Sunday and driving non-stop to get to the North West in time for practice on Tuesday night were tough, but they were manageable. After the North West was the Silverstone round of World Supersport, then straight back on a ferry to the Isle of Man for the TT.

Becky and me have never been much in debt. We're not into living beyond our means and that deal I did on the motorhome with Moodie was the only time I've ever really owed anyone anything. I was keen to get it paid off as soon as possible but at the same time get some start money in the bank for a mortgage. Doing the North West and the TT would help with that. I finished second to DJ at the 2002 TT, which left us with a bit of a lump.

I think it was back in 2000 that the taxman knocked on my door and gave me a bill for thirty grand. I fell over in a big heap. Ian Simpson, Jim Moodie and a few others had told me to keep receipts for absolutely everything and I had, but I didn't know what to do with them so I just kept them all in a bin liner. I had no idea when the man was going to come knocking, but I knew he'd do it one day. I was pointed in the direction of a cracking accountant, who I still use to this day. I held my hands up, gave him the bin liner full of receipts and he sorted it all out. That helped get me back in the system, which in turn helped in the hunt for a mortgage. Because I'm a bike racer, all the lenders wanted a massive deposit because of the risk involved. Luckily I had a decent lump of cash behind me and was able to put down what they were asking. We moved out of the camper and into a place in Morecambe in the middle of 2002.

*

I don't know if it was all the driving about and living on the road that caught up with me, but when it came to the fly-away round in Kyalami, I'd picked up a bit of a cold and felt like shit when I left for the airport. It was a two-hop flight which meant heading to Amsterdam and jumping on a long-haul flight down to South Africa. I felt worse and worse as the journey wore on. By the time I landed in Kyalami, I had what seemed to be a bad case of man flu. I tried to ignore it and cracked on, but it was hard work constantly sweating and not being able to eat.

By the time I did the track walk on the Thursday I was getting dizzy. I couldn't remember one corner from the next at walking pace, let alone riding the course.

On the Friday I rode the bike and threw up. I went out for the second session knowing that I was properly fucked. It was 25 degrees constantly, but I'd asked for extra duvets in the hotel room because I was freezing. I rang Becky at home and told her how bad I felt and she screamed at me to go and see a doctor but I just tried to crack on.

Then I went to the toilet and shat out white floaters. At that point I went to find the circuit doctor. The doc took one look at me and pulled my shirt up so he could listen to my chest. When I told him about the white poo, he said I had pneumonia and needed to be in hospital immediately. Within minutes of stumbling through the door, I was hanging upside down on a bed, having my lungs drained. They beat me like a dusty carpet, chasing the crap out of my lungs. I was jaundiced by then and had turned yellow because my liver had started shutting down. What began feeling like a cold landed me in hospital for four days because I'd ignored it and tried to be a man, like you do. I was wiped out while the race was happening, with massive needles in my stomach. I lost a couple of days in fact.

The team was scheduled to fly back on the Monday night and I was determined not to be left behind on my own so I signed myself out of hospital and joined them. By this stage I could barely talk, so it was hard for Becky to keep track of how I was until I got home. I soon picked up a bit, but I had no power or strength for a long time. It took me a couple of months to feel like I was over it.

CHAPTER 13

A Year to Forget

RACING-WISE, 2002 was a disaster. The Motorex Honda CBR 600 I was riding in World Supersport blew up everywhere. Monza, Assen, Donington, the TT, anywhere else you can think of, that bike let me down. It was the worst bike I've ever ridden. I quickly developed the skill of being able to tell within a lap when it would blow up. It was dreadful. I finished tenth on it in the 600 Production TT despite riding it really hard. I walked away wondering why I'd even bothered.

In the Supersport race, I was dicing for the lead with Jim Moodie, but in the Proddy race I was nowhere. I've often wondered why. Maybe the bike wasn't competitive or maybe it was something else. Either way, I got absolutely trounced. When I rode the 954 Fireblade in the 2002 production 1000 race to sixth place behind R1s and Suzukis, I was well happy. Compared to the R1 of the same era, the 954 Blade wasn't in the same street. It was pretty shit, to be fair. Luckily, they only made that model for a couple of years and we were able to move on to better things, but as it was it just couldn't touch the competition.

That year I was teammates with Karl Muggeridge and he was struggling with the same thing. You only have to look at how he turned things round in World Supersport when he joined Ten Kate Honda the following year to see the difference between a bad bike and a good one. He finished the 2002 season in 14th place; in 2003 he won three races and put the thing on pole twice. Karl was a great rider and when he came in and bounced his helmet off the garage walls in frustration, you knew that the job was fucked.

To top it off, I crashed a road bike filming with Steve Parrish at Croft, breaking my collarbone. I was still hurting when I went to Valencia that year and finished 19th. The team wouldn't take me to Australia for the race out there, blaming my collarbone, but in fact we'd run out of engines. The bottom line was the motors were being built wrongly and they just kept popping.

It got that bad that at the Silverstone round, the team leased a Ten Kate engine, told us all to keep quiet and put it in Karl's bike. They only leased the one of course, so I had to run with one of our grenade spec engines. I finished in 18th or something. Karl stuck the thing straight on the podium. The round before, we'd been running around together. It was complete bullshit.

I'd pleaded for a Ten Kate motor for the TT and didn't get one. I know with my hand on my heart I would have won a TT with a Ten Kate motor in that bike. I had one in my 2001 British Championship bike and it was fantastic. I had five poles and it was mega consistent. I offered to sign documents swearing me to secrecy if the team would sort me a Ten Kate motor for the TT but they just said no. At the TT, the 600 blew up as usual, but instead of it being on a nice safe circuit, this time it was at the end of the Cronk-y-Voddy Straight. When it went, I had a massive moment. The thing had thrown a rod and there was hot oil pissing all over the place. I immediately went sideways and became a passenger, I can remember thinking that I was about to die. I genuinely thought that the game was over.

I bounced off the grass bank and back into the road, and stopped the 600 as soon as I could. I don't think I've ever been as angry with a bike as I was that day. While I was screaming at it, I looked round and saw Iain Duffus seriously out of shape because of my spilled oil. His feet were off the pegs and he was all over the shop. They had to delay the next race while they cleaned up my mess. It was just shit. When I think about it now it pisses me off one minute and makes me want to cry the next. The Castrol Honda 600 I had the year before in the British Supersport would have been lovely at the TT but it was the foot-and-mouth year so it never happened.

When I look back over my career, 2002 is the year that I try to forget. The CBR600 that I'd ridden the previous year was so competitive that I could have won the British Supersport championship in the last round. It was down to me, Karl Harris and Kirk McCarthy. But my bike let go in the last round, so I finished in third place and Karl won it. There wasn't much other racing to focus on in 2001 because of the TT being cancelled and I really enjoyed the year in the British paddock. The only other race we did was Macau and I won there as well. I was having fun.

I was in good shape for 2002 but the dream ticket ride in World Supersport turned out to be a disaster from start to finish. I was on an uncompetitive bike that was tuned by a different outfit, on different tyres from the ones I was used to and in a paddock that I'd never been in, racing circuits that were new to me. Plus the pneumonia thing caught me out. I got off to a bad start and my bad luck didn't seem to change all year.

There were some good memories from that year, just not many to do with racing motorbikes. I travelled a lot, with Becky and baby Ewan, that part was brilliant. We used to go out three up on the scooter, me with the empty pushchair between my legs at the front and Ewan wedged in between me and Becky with a little plastic helmet on. We cruised into Misano like that in the boiling sun. We wouldn't dream of doing that now but it was fun back then. Unfortunately, the heat hung around for the race. It was 40 degrees on the day and totally unbearable. I was grateful for falling off on the third lap.

It didn't help that we hated the paddock. It was such a lonely place in comparison to the British paddock. We'd been mates with Neil Hodgson for years, but when he was racing he could be a grumpy bugger so it wasn't like I could knock the door on his camper for a beer. Karl Muggeridge was great, but treated everything he did so professionally that there wasn't much scope for a craic with him. Fair enough, I suppose. We got on really well with Colin Edwards, who won the World Superbike title that year. His wife Alyssia wasn't at every round but when she was, the four of us would convoy about together and stay at campsites in between rounds. Colin was the one I clicked with most. He'd think nothing of getting stuck into a bottle of wine to chill out of an evening. We're still mates now.

Nori Haga, Hodgy and a gaggle of the racers would all be there and things would chill out a bit once we were away from the circuit. James Toseland and Chris Walker were there but I never had any real banter with them.

It felt like the paddock was missing a hub where we could all meet, like we did in the British paddock. Well, there was one, but it was the sidecar boys. That's where I'd go if I wanted to disappear for an hour. There was always something funny going on with that lot.

They helped me when I drove to Monza, a place that feels like it's on the other side of the world. It lashed it down for most of the last day's driving. Becky and Ewan were sleeping while I was looking for the way into the circuit, which turned out to be a gate about the width of a single garage, in the middle of nowhere with no signs. I was driving round in circles trying to find the place and was running really low on diesel. I knew that once I was in and parked up, I could stick a few hundred litres of Ribena in tank that I had stored in the lockers of the camper.

I was stressing and swearing, then Becky woke up and started giving me aggro about finding the place and getting sorted out. It was a shitfest. When I finally found the way in, the motorhome died at the gate. I was out of fuel and blocking the entrance to the track. I had the beds up in seconds so that I could get at the motor. I stuck about 50 litres of Ribena in the thing and got Becky to turn it over while I bled the fuel system with the lift pump. There was shouting and screaming and I got a blister on my hand doing all the pumping, but it just refused to start.

Next thing, the sidecar boys tipped up, in the form of Steve Abbott and his passenger Jamie Biggs. Before I knew what was going on, one of them was cracking injectors with a 10mm spanner and we were running. I didn't ask for that help that day and they didn't need to give it, but they did and we hit it off immediately. I don't think you'd have caught a world championship-winning bike racer on his back in the pissing rain with a spanner in his hand. Sidecar lads love a problem to deal with.

So there were a few good memories to take away that year. I'd be telling my pals that I was at Misano, or Monza or Assen, racing in the world championship, and to them it sounded like everything I'd ever dreamed of, but in reality it was a massive disappointment. I didn't bother telling them about the fact that I usually only got about 30 minutes to figure out which way the track went before the bike blew up. Learn Assen in just half an hour of practice? Forget it. Nobody at world championship level runs at the front around a track they've never been to before. I came last at Monza for fuck's sake. Who wants to share that kind of news? To top off the misery, the depth of the field in the WSS Championship back then was insane. Fabien Foret, Charpentier, Kelner, MacPherson, Andrew Pitt and James Whitham were just a handful of the rapid guys.

The 600 market mattered back then and the top teams were getting proper factory backing. If you weren't on the pace, you were getting smoked. I qualified one second off pole at Oschersleben and that was me down in 20-something-th position. My best result all year was there: I finished 14th and bagged two points. I had a 15th at Silverstone and the same at that weird Grand Prix of Europe race at Brands Hatch. There must have been nearly a hundred thousand people there that weekend and it was mint, apart from the result of course. I think people call this kind of thing character building. I'm not sure I was calling it that when I was sitting in a camper that I owed twenty grand on after finishing out of the points in Misano.

In hindsight, a ride in the British Superbike championship might have been better. Anyway, eventually I got the sack. I missed the Sugo round so that I could race the TT and they replaced me with a Japanese rider called Tatsuya Yamaguchi. He crashed and broke his wrist.

I missed the Lausitzring because of road racing, so I was replaced again, and they gave me the flick for the last round at Imola in favour of Michael Laverty. I ended up doing the last round of the British Supersport championship on a private Honda and finished second to Scott Smart. Clearly I still had a bit of magic, I just couldn't find it on the bike I was riding in World Supersport. It ruined the dream of racing at World Championship level for me, but despite the bad luck I genuinely believe I wasn't good enough to win that year anyway. It was a tough field with some amazing guys on better machinery. I think if I'd had a year to learn the tracks and then another one to push on then maybe something good might have come of it. But if you weren't on top tackle, it was uphill from the start. I know that World Championship titles don't fall out of Christmas crackers, but this was bloody hard. I've no regrets for trying it, but walking away with less than five points for all that effort doesn't make me look back and smile.

CHAPTER 14

DJ

HONDA HAD LET me go at the end of the 2002 season and I went into 2003 with no real plans for anything. I ended up on my arse and lost a bit of momentum with my career. Handily, though, team managers knew there'd been a problem with the bike because the year before I'd been fighting for the British championship. Triumph and Jack Valentine stepped up in 2003 and it was great. I respect Triumph for pulling me out of the shit with that ride and was pleased when Bruce Anstey won the Junior 600 race for them. I also paid Paul Bird to ride his Monster Mob 998 Ducati in the big bike races. But 2003 wasn't all good news. It was the year we lost David Jefferies, and he was my best friend.

The man had a heart of gold. One time he got a bonus from a team in the shape of a brand new Suzuki GSX-R 1000. He could have sold it to fund his porn habit, or put the money into a trailer or some other project but he didn't. He gave it to a young lad he knew called Ian Hutchinson.

Dave helped Hutchy a lot at the start of Ian's career. They were local to each other and used to go on the piss together. Hutchy came onto the scene with a bit of a bang and Dave was happy to help him out with parts and bits and pieces to get him going. That was the kind of bloke he was. When it came to riding, Dave was fast but he was fair. He was always just that bit better than me and seemed to click with the big production bikes straight away, when I was struggling with them. I was just starting to get to grips with them when Dave was killed.

Our TT careers had gone down different paths since we both raced there for the first time in 1996. In 1997 he crashed a BMW at a press launch at Donington Park. He used to run a race-pattern gearshift on his bike and ended up on track on a bike with a road-pattern shift. He went the wrong way with a gear change, and high-sided himself into next week. He broke his collarbone and had to miss the TT that year. So by the end of 1997 I was a full TT ahead of him in terms of experience. I stuck with the little two-strokes and he established himself on the big bikes.

I'd like to have more early memories of riding with him on track at the TT, but to be honest I could never live with him. We were in different classes, but after evening practice, we'd end up together on track. He'd pass me on an R1 when I was on a 250 and I'd just be in awe of him. No matter where it was on track, he'd always pass me on the back wheel and there'd always be a big black line left. I know he'd have had that stupid big grin on his face as he went, laughing his head off. I just know it.

In 2000 he was strong. Foot-and-mouth meant no TT in 2001, as I've said. He dominated in 2002 and was killed the following year. I don't think he was in the best place in his head in 2003. I never totally understood what and why, but he started the year having a bad time with his partner, Susan. They lived quite far apart and his mind was either fixed on building trailers or on tits. Becky and me really liked Susan, lots of people did and they seemed great together, but Dave ended up with a new bird. We were a bit shocked, but it wasn't really our business. I thought that as long as he was happy that was OK.

Aside from the Tyco ride that he had, he was struggling to find a bike to race in 2003. The man was a multiple national Superstock champion and ended up running in the British paddock on his own bike, pretty much on his tod. My good mate Mick painted Dave's bike for him, then he came and stayed at mine and the three of us prepped his bike together. I think he was puzzled about why he was in that position. I'm not sure how much the bike and girl situation was playing on his mind, but he didn't seem the Dave we all knew. He wanted a superbike ride in BSB more than anything and that didn't look like it was going to happen, despite the way he had dominated Superstock.

He went off to the North West and was on the pace. He had a win in one race and his bike broke down in another, but he was there. At the TT in 2003 he was struggling a little bit in practice, his set-up wasn't quite there on the TAS Suzuki. He'd dominated on that bike the year before, setting a lap record of 127.29mph. Dave isn't here to defend himself and it feels awkward talking about his personal situation, but like I said, I thought that his head wasn't quite right because of his women troubles. Maybe he was thinking that he'd made a mistake and that he still loved Susan, who knows? Anyway, he was looking for a set up that worked and ended up going back to an old one that he just clicked with. Lo and behold, he did a 125mph standing start lap, the fastest in practice. Then, three miles into his second lap he was killed.

I know he was on a good lap and I know he would have been happy with what was going on. He would have been smiling, hitting the spots on a bike that was going well. One minute the penny had dropped and everything was tickety boo. Then he was gone in a breath.

I remember we were messing about on the start line that day. There was no real structure to practice week and whoever got to the front first got away and had clear track. Adrian Archibald and DJ were the first two away and I wanted to go with him to see if I could hang with him and learn something on the MonsterMob Ducati I was riding. Dave elbowed me out of the way when we were paddling our bikes to the start line and him and Archie were gone. Ten seconds later Jim Moodie and me were away. Jim was on the little Triumph. I got away from him and chased and chased to try to catch the leading two. There was no way I was going to do it, they were gone.

I put the crash down to oil on the track and always will. Some people beg to differ, but I was the first man on the scene and saw it with my eyes. He'd probably taken ten seconds out of me, plus the ten-second gap he had from the start. Crosby is nigh on flat out, you just roll on the way in and then you're straight back into sixth gear. You are tramming along through there.

I saw a yellow flag and just assumed someone had broken down, but something stopped me and made me slow right down. You can knock 80mph off your speed round that place and still be doing a hundred. I kept reducing speed off and it just didn't feel right.

Then I saw a woman in the crowd who'd taken her red coat off and was waving it at me. I thought I was cracking up. I wasn't sure if she was even real. Even months afterwards I still couldn't compute if I'd actually seen a woman waving a red coat at the side of the road or not. I said so during the inquest and it turned out she was real because she was there. I couldn't believe it. The bottom line is that it doesn't really fucking matter as Dave's gone, but it confirmed that the women had done what I thought she'd done. Fair play to her, if she'd walked up and poked me in the eye I wouldn't have recognised her, but I do genuinely thank that lady. She showed some initiative and could have stopped something even more horrendous from happening.

It was almost funny, when I came across the crash site and stopped. All I saw in the middle of the road was a perfect seat unit. The bike went on to do whatever it did but it popped the seat off and it was sitting in the road with that big number one on it. Dave's visor was next to it. I try and blank out the rest of it because it was carnage, but it won't go away.

The engine was in the road, there were brake discs, bits of exhaust packing and bent metal scattered around, and oil, steam and fucking smoke everywhere. It was hideous but Dave was laid out perfectly like he was having a sleep. People say his boot had come off but it hadn't. Nevertheless, the impact was so severe that it knocked his dog tag off. They found it in a garden. How the hell can you knock one of those off? His family got it back, I'm pleased to say, which was amazing.

I leant my Ducati against the wall and remember the sound of it idling away while I looked about. I turned the bike off and it was silent for a second, then I could hear more bikes approaching fast. 'Oh for fuck's sake,' I thought. I could see that things might be about to get worse.

There was a fireman there called Big H, who had clearly seen lots of scenes like this one in his time. He saw me sitting on the wall. He picked me up with a Fireman's lift and just carried me away. We sat round the corner and he told me there was nothing I could do and that we should leave the job to the guys that knew what they were doing. I could hear the air ambulance coming. I'd stopped, so had Farquhar, Richard Britton and quite a few others. Jim Moodie had come round the corner and got tangled up with the telephone wire across the road from the pole that Dave brought down when he crashed – it nearly had Jim's head off. I can still hear the horrible noise that wire makes when it's stretching, in my head now. It was all like something out of a Hollywood movie. It had to have been scripted to be as bad as it was.

Afterwards, when my head was in bits, David's mum, Pauline Jefferies said to me that he would have wanted me to carry on and race. I felt horrible and didn't know what to say to anyone. I said that I was ready to go home and she just told me to carry on and that everything would be okay. Everyone in the paddock seemed to have remained upbeat and happy. I can remember thinking 'Fuck me, what the hell is going on here?'

There are a lot of strong people in racing and not all of them are the ones who ride the bikes. The Jefferies family are great examples of this. I'm still pals with DJ's dad, Tony, and his sister Loubie.

Ever since that day, I've found it hard to get friendly with people. Whenever I meet someone new, I think about how I don't want to get too close to them in case anything happens. Some really inspirational people have been hurt and killed road racing over the years. Gus Scott getting killed in 2005 was one example, Mick Lofthouse and Pullan were others. Gavin Lee was a good mate of mine too, he was killed in 1999 at the Southern 100. Then somebody else, then another one. I'm left thinking, 'what the fuck?' But you go back, don't you? I'm not into drugs and I never have been, but the cliché about road racing being like a drug rings true in my head. There is just something about it that drags me in. It's like a magnet on my body and it won't let go of me.

Off track, there aren't many people in the sport like Dave. He was a Northern lad like me, with similar interests. Bit of scrambling, a bit of Supermoto, a bit of this and that, with pizza and a pie after a good day out on the bikes. We were so alike, that's why we hit it off. We just complemented each other's characters. Like me, DJ didn't feel the need to train. Neil Hodgson is a good mate of mine but he was obsessed with training. Dave didn't bother. It just happened for him and I don't think he cared that much either. As long as he was doing skids and wheelies, if he finished second or third it was what it was. He didn't take himself too seriously, but he did have a gift for riding bikes. And he wasn't always out on the piss or chasing birds and shagging. He just got blinded by tits, that's all.

Up until that day in 2003 Dave was dominating the TT. He was a winning machine and I would love to know where he would have gone with it if he wasn't killed. He did nine wins in three years and was out of everyone's reach. When I was doing 125mph laps, he was doing 127s. That's a country mile of a gap. I was finishing second to him, but I was a minute and a half behind him across the line. And he was pulling fucking wheelies for the crowd while he was dominating.

His sister Loubie would run his pit board for him out of the Creg and he'd make sure to pull a massive fifth-gear wheelie for her every time he went past. He was enjoying himself, as well as taking it seriously. It didn't matter if it was damp, or if it was pissing with rain, he was quick. I'd be shitting myself sometimes if the weather wasn't right or the conditions were sketchy. I can remember seeing Dave on dry tyres in BSB, leading in the rain. He had a natural feel for a motorbike and it didn't matter what sort it was. He had a magic touch and had a lot of success that people forget about. He rode in the Aprilia 250 Challenge when he was about 16 stone and the bike looked like it had been wedged up his arse. It didn't matter to Dave, he'd race anything anywhere, usually to the podium as well.

The side of him that people might not have seen would come out in things like how excited he would get over his toolbox at home. He must have had twenty grand's worth of Snap On tools in his garage, and he loved it. I miss both sides of David. I think my son does as well, despite him having only been a baby when Dave was about. He'd always park up near to us and take Ewan off in the pram for a walk round the paddock, or he'd lift him onto his shoulders and go and have a hike around whatever circuit we were at. They had a connection.

I don't want to speak out of turn, but sometimes something massive has to happen for things to change. If rider 56 had crashed on that oil and was killed, I reckon the TT would be exactly the same now as it was then. But the oil took the number one guy out. The fucking number one guy. Because of that, everyone asked why.

His results will go down in history, but Dave's death also had a massive impact on the TT. Marshalling changed and the safety systems improved. You can't make that place completely safe, we know that. But if there's any doubt now, a flag goes up. I'm brilliant at putting on my blinkers and ignoring the bad stuff, but the end result was that Dave was gone.

I went to the inquest and was numb as fuck. I was listening to people talking shit and wanted to jump the barrier and rip the fucking coroner's eyes out. I thought he was a patronising arsehole. I remember listening to him saying '180 miles an hour, on a road!' and then looking around the room for a reaction, like we were all deranged lunatics. I felt that he was as good as saying that we were fucking idiots. I thought he was a prick. We are professionals. Our riding at the TT has helped develop brake pads and tyres, and has contributed to making bikes better and safer.

I had my turn in the stand and was cross-examined. They kept asking me, 'Was there oil on the track?' I said yes. They asked me so many times that I ended up questioning myself. I've never been in that situation before and it was strange how they were able to do that. There was no doubt in my mind though and I said as much. They left it at that. I don't know what they wanted me to say.

The verdict they returned was death by misadventure. So if I'd have said there was an eight-foot dildo on the track or a fucking 12-foot crocodile crossing it, it wouldn't have made any difference. For me that woman in the red coat saved me that day. Even if it sounds selfish to say so because David is gone.

*

If I shut my eyes and think about David Jefferies my pal rather than DJ the TT racer, the first thing I picture is him doing doughnuts in his truck in the paddock at Oulton Park. I can see him hanging out the window laughing his head off while Suzy screams at him to stop. Glen Richards and somebody else are in the passenger seat and there's fucking smoke everywhere. Listening to this truck being tortured is deafening, but Dave is laughing. He was still laughing when he skidded over a cable and knocked out the power to the whole paddock.

When I think about DJ the TT racer, I see him edging away from me in the distance with a big black line coming off his Pirelli tyre. He's on the back wheel of the V&M R1 and his fat arse is hanging off. He's using that extra ingredient, that little piece of something that I just didn't have at the time. I'm frustrated and completely in awe of what he's doing.

We always wondered if he was pushing too hard. But he'd come in and jump off his bike and there wouldn't be a drop of sweat. He was never blowing out of his arse. It was easy for him, he was never nervous and was always taking things to the next level. When I was flapping before a race, Dave would just be taking the piss. He was made from different gravy from everyone else. He had no kids as well, he didn't leave a massive trail of aggro behind him when he died which I always think makes things easier for everyone.

He left a few bikes and his tools which needed to be sorted. I bought his Supermoto spec Honda CRF from his dad, along with a tent and a few other bits and pieces to remind me of him. His dad was happy that I did that. I've won a few races on that Honda since I bought it in 2003 and would never part with it. There'll always be part of Dave with me whatever happens, he was a special character and there isn't anyone like him in the sport now.

*

It was a difficult time for me. My career was going down a route I didn't understand. I rode Birdy's Ducati that year but because I wasn't contracted to a team, I had to go and find a sponsor to pay the five grand entry fee. I rode a Triumph and was there in terms of pace, but I was all over the place in terms of organisation. I badly wanted to win the race in 2003, to dedicate it to Dave, but his teammate Adrian Archibald won it. It was fitting for the team, really.

I didn't have much sorted in advance for 2004. The year before, I'd bagged my third TT win, on the 400cc Honda in the lightweight race. I'd finished tenth and 18th on the 600cc Triumph at the TT and second and third on Birdy's MonsterMob Ducati. I'd also ridden the ETI Ducati at the North West.

But I was all over the bloody place at the start of 2004. David Jefferies' death must have had an impact on me, even if I'd tried to block it out. I wasn't able to just move on and I lost momentum again because I didn't have a deal tied down with one manufacturer for the whole season.

CHAPTER 15

Yamaha

ONE THURSDAY MORNING I was at home, mowing my lawn and minding my own business, when the phone rang. It was Gus Scott. He said 'Get yourself to Le Mans as fast as you can.' He was racing out there at the 24 hour in a three-man team with Johnny Barton and Andy Notman. Andy had crashed in practice and done his collarbone. The team were stuck for a rider and I was scratching my arse at home doing nothing. Gus said I had to be there by the Friday morning. I didn't think twice, I just said, 'alreet, I'll see you in the morning', and hung up the phone.

Gus was a good mate of mine. He was right on my wavelength. It's very hard to find someone like that, somebody who can read me and know where my head is at all the time. He was from Kendal, which isn't far from me. Gus was a motorcycle journalist, but he was also a fucking good bike rider. He was fast. Making the Superstock podium in BSB in the early 2000s was tough but Gus managed it. He was respected by readers and racers. Like lots of others, I loved the way he wrote.

I dumped the mower back in the garage, filled the boot of my BMW 318 diesel with clobber and set off for Dover to catch a ferry. I drove all day and night and by the time I got to Le Mans it was ridiculous o'clock in the morning. I grabbed a few hours' sleep in my car and just after breakfast on the Friday morning I was out on the bike for free practice. We qualified and that was it, we were going endurance racing.

The bike was a Kawasaki ZX-10R prepped and owned by Alf's Kawasaki down in Worthing. It was a new model that had just come out that year. It went on to have a bit of a bad-boy reputation on the road but as an endurance racer it was fine.

We did all right, finishing eighth or something. I've still got the trophy in the house. We weren't particularly fast as a team but we enjoyed the experience. I didn't set out with any real endurance racing aspirations and just treated it as a run out. I got to tick a box in racing terms and I also got to watch Gus doing ten pumper wheelies down the finishing straight during his stints on the bike.

When I jumped in the car, Becky and a mate of mine hopped on a plane to France and met me down there. That's what we do. When we finished, me and Becky jumped in the car and drove home with a couple of quid in my pocket that I used to put fuel in the car, and that was that. I left home with nothing and got home with nothing but a trophy and the knowledge that I'd raced the 24 Hours at Le Mans. Like I said before, money is important but it doesn't mean everything to me.

Endurance racing reminds me of that spaced-out, jet laggy feeling you get in Macau. Walking down to a track to do a stint at three o' clock in the morning when the rest of the world is asleep. When you've had an hour's sleep in the last 15, your mind starts to play games with you and you have to fight with yourself to stay alert. There's no better way to wake up though. Someone shakes you awake at six in the morning and you fall into your leathers and onto a bike feeling like someone's thrown cement in your eyes. Then you get the chance to experience the sun coming up while you're flat out on a bike. As tired as you may be, it's special.

*

You rarely hear people talking about my Yamaha days at the TT from that era, but personally I'm proud of them. I rode well on those bikes and they played their part in my story. I'll never forget how well Yamaha treated me. Andy Smith was fantastic. He used to be the big boss at Yamaha UK and is now the Vice President of sales for Yamaha Europe. Him and me put together a one-meet deal in 2004. Yamaha paid me 20 grand to ride the new R1, which was good money back then. All they wanted to do was give me a superbike for the Formula One and the Senior TT races. No North West, just TT and more TT. Rob Mac and his team built the bike, but I had to organise the rest of my TT effort myself.

Graham Hanna from a company called IFS helped. Graham was a proper bloke, a really solid and trustworthy businessman. He was successful but fair and was brilliant with me. I still do a bit for him wherever I can and I'll always be massively grateful for the help he gave me in 2004. He'd had 600cc Hondas built for me and I just went into his house and asked him to change everything to Yamahas, even though I barely knew him. He said 'no problem, John' and built me new 600cc Yamahas. I delivered the results for him, winning the North West and the TT Junior 600, but I was shitting myself a little bit after making the demands. Like I said, those results crept under the radar a little bit but they're massive to me.

I ended up going to a shop called Keith Dixon Yamaha in Accrington and buying their road-legal demonstrator R1 off the showroom floor with my own money. I finished second on it in the production race. I could have won it: I was there in terms of pace but I ran out of fuel.

I also bought my own stock 600 Yamaha R6, prepped it and finished on the podium in the 600 proddy race as well. It was a great year. The Superbike was the priority, though, and if the clutch hadn't bust, I could have won six races. But if my auntie had a cock she'd be my uncle, and there's no use looking back saying I could have done this or that. With Dave missing it felt empty and the mainstream press seemed to be doing nothing but focusing on the death and danger element of the TT, rather than the racing and the winning.

The wins felt great to me and they can never be taken away, but I just wish Dave had been there. I'd definitely sacrifice some of the TT wins I've had for some more time with him. I'd like to have tried to beat him round the Isle of Man. I beat him at Macau and Scarborough but they don't come close to the TT. He was always one gear ahead of me round there. Whether I could have caught him, I don't know, but I felt pretty invincible on the Yamaha in 2004. I smoked Archibald, who'd won the year before, and I was fast. I also beat Dave's lap record, only by a touch mind. We'll never know if Dave would have come back in 2004 and had a 128mph lap in him.

*

I went into 2004 feeling like I needed a manager to make sure things happened when they were supposed to. I rang Jim Moodie and said I was calling in the favour he owed me and that he had to come to the TT to help me.

Up until then I'd never been properly mentally prepared for TT racing. I was always up late or in the pub. I wasn't sharp and was more than happy to be the 20th or 30th bike away in practice. I was lazy and needed somebody to whip me into shape. Jim took care of all that, preparing the bike so it was all ready to go and doing the simple things that you don't think matter until you get them right, like making sure I always had water.

Nowadays the seeded riders get away first in practice but back then it was a free-for-all. A newcomer could get off the line before everyone else if he got to the front of the queue. Jim Moodie would push everyone out of the way and get my bike to the front. He didn't mess about. I'd do two laps on the big bike and go into the pit, where he'd have my 600 and a fresh visor waiting for me, and I'd be straight back out. Spare helmet and a drink, with spare knee sliders if I needed them and tyre warmers being slipped off at just the right moment. It was great and it showed how unorganised I'd been up until then. Jim dotted the i's and crossed the t's.

I'd always got on well with Jim, and we worked well together. He tried to get me training in the gym and it did feel like it was having an effect but I got fed up of going. He ran his training with a bit of an iron fist, which was okay but probably a little too much for me.

In 2004 I absolutely dominated the TT. I only won three races, but I led in everything else. I know Hutchy won five in 2010, but at one stage or another I was ahead in everything.

I was leading the 600 production race when my steering damper broke. I was in front in the 1000 production race until I ran out of fuel. I was leading the Senior by 40 seconds until the clutch started slipping. I still won three races though and it was a real turning point. Within four laps of practice I'd done a 127.68mph lap on the big Yamaha and had broken David Jefferies' record. Then I broke it again in the race itself, setting a record that I held until Bruce Anstey took it in 2014. (When that happened I took it back the following year and then lost it again in 2016).

After the TT I had nothing sorted. When the phone rang and I was given the chance to replace Glen Richards on the Hawk Kawasaki, I jumped at it. Glen had crashed at Thruxton and smashed his elbow, so I stepped in. Before I knew it, I was on the podium at Brands Hatch in BSB with John Reynolds and Sean Emmett. Talk about zero to hero. Suddenly I'm in everyone's face again and getting my momentum back. After the patchy 2003 and 2004 TT season, it felt good to have a solid ride secured with Hawk Kawasaki until the end of 2004 in the BSB.

*

In 2005 I'd sorted a deal riding for Vivaldi Potatoes. The team owner was a bit up and down. He told me I wasn't allowed any sponsors at all and that he'd pay me. He told me I had to wear an Arai without any Arai stickers on it, which was weird. I didn't have anything else going on, so I agreed. Then Yamaha came along with the Aim Yamaha deal for 2005.

I was in the car park at the Birmingham NEC bike show in 2004, still trying to figure out which way to go. Inside, there was my Vivaldi ZX-10 with John McGuinness written on it. That's how close we were to unveiling the bike and the new team to the public. I cocked on the deal in the morning at the very last minute. I wanted to work with Yamaha and Jim Moodie, who was going to run the team for me like he had done in 2004.

The Yamaha seemed like the way forward. There was money coming in from Aim as a sponsor, and Shoei helmets had offered me good deal as well. Yamaha were also happy for me to do my other bits and pieces, whereas the Vivaldi guy wanted to control everything. It just felt right. It was a horrible having to tell a team I was out at the last minute. I never want to be in that situation again. A man's word is a man's word, and that means a lot to me. But sometimes the cards that life deals need to be thrown back on the table. Tight as it was, it felt like the right thing to do.

I rang Ben Wilson's dad Richard, who was going to run the ZX-10s for the team. I said that I was outside in the car park and that I was going to have to cock out on the deal. It was half an hour before the doors for the show were due to open, when the general public would see our bike for the upcoming year. I just said that I was really sorry but I was going to go with what Yamaha had offered. I didn't know what else to say. To be fair, Richard completely understood. He was a normal working-class man like me and he could see why I was doing what I was doing.

The big boss from Vivaldi who was bank-rolling the whole thing went nuts and demanded a meeting. I had to be a man and go to it. I sat there, getting absolutely dressed down by this little fat Italian guy. Half of me wanted to tell him to go and get fucked because of what he was calling me. He was the boss of a multi-million pound company and was clearly used to getting what he wanted. He was not happy, but at the same time I could understand his frustrations and knew that I had to take the bollocking and move on. I sat there like a kid, getting ten tons of abuse over the table while he smashed his hand into it. 'Nobody fucking does this to me!' he was shouting. I just stared at the floor. My mind was made up and I wanted to go with Yamaha.

In hindsight, I had a fairly disastrous year with them. We didn't get the results we were looking for in BSB, I was running at the edge of the top ten and was scratching my head a bit. BSB isn't easy, there were some great riders on some factory bikes. We just got on with the job and worked as hard as we could.

CHAPTER 16

Hong Kong Dollars

IT WAS PISSING it down during the North West and one of the races was cancelled. But I was sharp for the TT and it was mega. We blitzed everyone in both the Senior and the Superbike races by over thirty seconds. It wasn't all good though. 2005 was the year in which I had what was probably my biggest moment at the TT that didn't involve crashing.

To do a great lap at the TT, you have to get straight back in if you have a moment. You can't afford to roll off and have a breather. You have moments pretty much everywhere, but you know most of them are coming. You're aware there might be a bit of a tank-slapper here or a slide there. Tyres start to go off or you land a jump hard on the gas, but you're only a little bit out of shape and the bike shakes its head at you. I can keep the throttle in when that happens. What really spooks you are the ones you don't see coming. For me the biggest and scariest moment I know I'm going to have is a tank-slapper that I always get in the same place. It was there that I had my biggest ever moment at the TT, in practice on the 600 Supersport bike in 2005.

Just after Kerrowmoar there's a long right, left, right before the council yard. I was on the crown of the road when something happened and I got into a tank-slapper. Lock to lock to lock, over and again. I was pinned in top gear and the bike was going crazy underneath me. The fairing was smashed off and my right foot was sucked under the back wheel with so much force that my leg bent the rear brake lever back on itself.

Now, we've all heard people saying that if you get into a tank-slapper you should just accelerate out of it. Those guys who tell you that in the pub are talking shit. When a bike is banging off the lock stops, the thing to do is immediately start praying to the big man above. I was a passenger on that 600 for about 300 yards, completely out of control with strange involuntary animal noises coming out of my mouth. Fuck me I was scared. Somehow I came out of it but I have no idea how, so Christ knows how your pal up the pub knows the solution. The bodywork was smashed, the clocks were hanging off, the brake lever was pointing at the rear wheel and I'd run myself over without actually crashing. That's how violent it was.

Even to this day, whatever bike I'm riding, I can't completely predict what the bike is going to do through there. I wonder if I go tense through that section, which might be making things worse, or if I freeze. I don't know. I've been through it in the car and got out and studied the road but I had no idea what I was looking for. That moment was horrible, on a 600 of all things. It wasn't the low point of the 2005 TT though, not by a long shot.

*

Losing Gus Scott was tough and it was made worse by the fact that I sprayed Champagne on the podium in the Senior race that he was killed in without knowing he was gone. I wouldn't have celebrated the win if I had known. It looked like I had no respect for him but I totally did. I just didn't know what had happened. I'd seen his bike parked up at the side of the road in the race and assumed he'd broken down. It was only after the podium that I found out.

After what happened to Gus, I don't like giving people advice about the TT. I'd told him to come over and do it because I knew he'd be safe as houses round there. He would have been, but a marshal walked out in front of him and he died as a result. It wasn't my fault and it wasn't Gus's, but I'll feel guilty about it until the day I die. I went to the funeral and I could see in their faces that his mum and dad blamed motorbikes for Gus's death. That's why it's frustrating now when I hear younger lads saying that racing the TT is on their bucket list. They need preparation.

That's one of the reasons why I waited as long as I did before I started racing on the Isle of Man. I could easily have saved some money by skipping races at home, come over on my TZ and done it on a wing and a prayer. But it would have been a nightmare. I wasn't prepared and I was too young. I know that lots of people struggle to get there because of money, but you need new kit for the TT. People go with motors that make massive horsepower and end up learning nothing because they're spending all their time fixing them rather than riding as many laps as possible. I've offered this small piece of advice to a few guys at the Manx and don't really care if they have chosen to take it or not. I know what's needed, I just do.

*

Not long after the 2005 TT, Yamaha and me parted company again. It wasn't working for me in BSB and I wasn't enjoying it. When we finished at Knockhill I told the team that I was going. Jim Moodie had ended up smacking one of the mechanics and leaving the team. Things weren't happening how I wanted them to. They were trying and I was trying but we just couldn't make things work between us. It wasn't a handshake and a mutual thing when we split. I fell out with Alistair Flanagan, who was the team boss. It was a shitty way to end it. I ended up riding the Vitrans Honda in BSB when they let John Laverty go as well. Ian Simpson ran it and I stayed with them until the end of the 2005 season. I was still seat-hopping though – I ended up back on Birdy's Stobart-sponsored bike for the Ulster Grand Prix and Macau. I felt all over the place.

*

The money that I used to win at Macau was only ever a couple of hundred quid in cash, always paid in Hong Kong dollars. I'd spend a bit of it out there and take the change home. Some years I'd win more than others. I thought it'd be a good idea to save what I took home, put it in a bag and forget about it. The plan was that when I'd finished my Macau racing career I could count it all up and buy something that would remind me of why I raced there. Something that I'd never part with. I'd always fancied a massive home cinema set-up. Proper seats like you get at the movies, bullshit surround sound and a massive projector.

I'd been saving and hiding this money in a bin bag in the back of the garage for 11 or 12 years and must have had about four grand in cash in it when I accidentally threw it out with the rubbish. I can laugh about it now, but when I realised what I'd done I was raging, I ripped my garage to bits looking for the bag but I must have been having a clean-out one time and accidentally added it to the rubbish. I still sometimes wonder if it's hidden somewhere in the garage and I just can't find it, but I know it's gone really and that hurts. It took me a good week or two to get over that one. I'd forget about it, then remember, get that sinking horrible feeling in my guts and have to sit down.

An even better story about me being stupid with money is the time I bought myself an E46 BMW M3 in 2005. The TT job was going all right, I had a couple of good contracts flying about and I was living the dream. We didn't really need a family car so I thought, 'Bollocks to it, I'm getting an M3'.

I saw the one I wanted on eBay and got in touch with the owner, who lived in Rushden. I said I'd bring a banker's draft with me and if the car was as advertised, I'd pay for it and drive it home there and then. I took one of my mates with me and we met these skinheads in a pub. As soon as I saw them I thought they were going to kick my head in and do one with my money. They looked nasty.

We had a quick drink and they said they'd take me to this little unit where the car was locked up. I was convinced it was going to go wrong. We followed them down all these back lanes in the pitch black. When we pulled up at the unit I was already preparing to get filled in. One of the guys went in, opened the big door and flicked on the light. I took one look at the car and handed over the draft. Turned out the seller was genuine and the car was too. He pulled out a full service history, told me he thought the tyres were a bit crappy and we had a good chat. The car was beautiful. Phoenix yellow with black leather, a Harman Kardon stereo and all the toys. It even had an M3 number plate. I thought the thing was ace.

I drove it around for about six months, then a car dealer mate of mine said he'd buy it from me for slightly more than I'd paid for it. As we shook on the deal, I reminded myself of my dad when I was a kid. He would always take a profit for a toy as well. When I dropped the M3 off at my pal's dealership, he gave me a cheque and about £1,200 in readies in an envelope. I jumped in a mate's car and drove off.

When I got home, I realised that I'd put the envelope on the roof of the car before I got in. It was gone, obviously. While I was smiling away thinking I'd won on the deal, twelve hundred quid was blowing down the road. I was devastated. But I made somebody happy that day. Imagine finding handfuls of cash in the street. I've convinced myself that whoever found it needed it more than I did. A family with nothing or a kid who was in the shit. Not just somebody who would piss it against the wall, but we'll never know.

*

Despite the hectic season I had in 2005, I knew there was some good things coming in 2006. Midway through the year, Honda racing boss Neil Tuxworth called me for a catch-up. When he mentioned that he'd be at the Southern 100 to ride in a parade lap, I said I'd be there too, to watch the racing and see a few of the lads. Racing at the Southern has never appealed to me. Neil suggested we should meet up. A couple of weeks later, I ended up in his car in Castletown, where he pulled out a deal and stuck it in front of me. It was okay money, but it also covered racing in the British Superstock championship, the North West, the TT and everything I wanted. I only jumped in his car for a chat and didn't see it coming at all.

I'd be riding in the HM plant colours with Karl Harris and Ryuichi Kiyonari. They also had Jonathan Rea and Eugene Laverty in the Red Bull team. It was a big, professional outfit. I just thought, 'What else can I do? I have to do this.' I signed a letter of intent there and then in the car for a two-year deal, opened the door and walked away with a big smile on my face. 2005 had been a bit of a hit and miss season. It was great to know that I'd be back on the Honda train. I always thought that if you were handy on the short circuits and fast on the roads then the door would open at Honda. I was ready to go for it in Superstock in the British paddock, I had what I wanted for the roads and I would be working with Leighton Haigh and Julian Boland to get the bikes how I wanted them, two great guys who I still work with now. It was a combination made in heaven, really, and it felt ace.

If I'd had a personal manager or somebody advising me, maybe I could have got another ten or 20 grand. But I was after some structure and direction and this deal seemed to offer both. That was in 2006 and I'm still with Honda 11 years later. My career seemed to go from almost nothing to back on track in a heartbeat. It wasn't until this point that I got the kind of structure to the race effort that fans don't see, the bits where you're running around sorting sponsors and bikes and all the behind-the-scenes stuff that people don't think about when they're cheering you on.

Andy Smith from Yamaha sent me a lovely letter and six bottles of Champagne at the end of the year. Even though I'd gone to Honda, he still wished me well. They were good people at Yamaha and I'll never forget that.

CHAPTER 17

Lucky Socks

MY PROCESS OF preparation for the TT has evolved over the years. Since the first time I raced there, I don't think there has been a day when I didn't think about where I'm going to be on the track. Am I going to be competitive? Who is going to get what start number? I don't plan to think about it. It just enters my mind and I immediately feel something in my body, like I've had an electric shock. It's like a nervous twitch.

Over the years, I've learned to surround myself with the right people and to be on the right bike, with the right tyres. These things have a cumulative effect. It's changed a bit now, but from 2006 to 2011 it happened without me really realising it. I had the same bike and the same mechanics, which meant I wasn't on the phone trying to cover the bases. I was sorted because the people surrounding me knew how I clicked and ticked.

Guy Martin jumped from Aim Yamaha to SMR Honda to TAS Suzuki, then BMW. Pirellis to Dunlops, then back again. Things were never settled and although he's had success at the Ulster Grand Prix, he still hasn't achieved the ultimate win he's chasing. For me, the best preparation was to find an overall set-up that couldn't break, so we didn't have to fix it. This gave me peace of mind and because of that stability, I believed that I could beat them all. On my day, I can, and I often wonder if those boys lined up on race day thinking that I was unbeatable. I certainly wanted them to. Winning is about keeping one step ahead of everyone all time, which means being fastest in practice. That's what I always aim for.

I know that my way has probably infuriated a lot of people who have trained really hard, only to see me do things my way and win, but by keeping everything simple and not overcomplicating things, I'm able to focus purely on what matters most: riding fast every time I get on the bike.

*

I rode fast in 2006, that's for sure. I won three TTs, blitzed the Superbike, the Senior and the Supersport races, and pushed the lap record to 129.4mph in the Senior. I felt great that my deal with Honda had stepped off on the right foot. I was happy with my performances away from the TT as well. I finished in the top ten in the British Superstock championship, the only Honda rider to do so in a year when Suzukis were really strong.

This was also the year that Paul Phillips started turning the TT around, he was employed by the government on the Isle of Man as the development guy for the whole event. It had been bouncing along the bottom for a good few years and needed a proper shake-up to reach a new audience. Paul still does the job now and has helped turn the TT into a bit of a monster publicity wise. Thirty million people will watch the racing on telly all over the world in 2017 – crazy numbers.

*

I have a fair few superstitions that I've picked up along the way. I always mow the lawn before I leave for the island. It's like a woman tidying up the house before someone comes round. I always thought that mowing the lawn would be one less thing for Becky to do when she got home from the TT if anything went wrong. It's bizarre and a bit pathetic really, but superstitions do that to you. They don't make a shite of a difference to the result, but it feels right so I do it. When I'm on the start line and I know everything is neat and tidy at home, I feel I'm ready to go and can get on with the job.

I've insisted on having a voodoo doll painted on my helmet since I won at Daytona in 2000. I went out there with the first custom-painted helmet I'd ever owned, Ali Grant from Bike Paints in Scotland did it and I felt like a dog with two dicks. It was all pink and blue swirls, with my name on the back. It made me feel ace. Then I crashed in practice and smacked my head on the ground, which wrote the helmet off.

We were sharing a garage at the track with a guy called Jack Silverman, who gave me one of his to race in. Jack was an artist, but he had his own race team as well, and combined the two passions by hand-painting helmets. Why would anybody want to paint a hundred Arai helmets with a different item from his art collection on each one? Bizarre things, vases, rugs, Zulu shields, all kinds of weird shit. Anyway, Jack gave me the one of the hundred which had the Voodoo doll on it. I won the race, then I won everything else that year, TT and British Championship. I've never raced in a helmet without that symbol on it since.

I've recently added the need to race in a pair of socks with 'Daddy' written on them. I started that when the kids came along and somebody got me them for Christmas. Whenever I'm on two wheels, I have to wear them. When I'm pulling them on, I'm not thinking about how they can give me an edge to win, I'm thinking about the family connection with the people who gave them to me and how I want to stay safe enough to see them again. The Voodoo on my helmet is there for success, but the socks, they're a safety measure! My kids mean more to me than any race win.

About ten or 12 years ago, my son Ewan found a coin and gave it to me for luck so I started putting that down my leathers. We've changed the coin a few times. If I've been having a shit day on the bike or haven't got the result I was after, I tell the kids to find me another coin and they do. I found one outside Steve Plater's motorhome in 2009. It was right by his steps and I told him it was going to bring me luck for the first race. When I won it, we jokingly questioned whether or not it was down to the coin. That's what superstitions are all about, I suppose.

CHAPTER 18

One Rider and One Lap 130mph

I'VE HEARD SOME riders talk about how their fastest lap at a track is normally the one that feels the slowest. For me it both is and it isn't like that. It's hard to explain. In 2007 I was doing high 128mph laps in practice and I felt mint. The weather was good, I was getting off the bike feeling fresh, with no sweat or puffing, and I just felt strong. I stepped into the motorhome and told Becky that I was going to go for it. I was going to push for a 130mph lap record; at the time was mine at 129mph. 2007 was the centenary year and I was going to show everyone that I was the daddy.

That night in practice I got off on a flyer on the standing start lap and really went for it on the second lap. I thought I was doing it at 180mph, I was absolutely flying. I came in sweating, blowing out of my ring piece but expecting the big number and a cheer form everyone. It wasn't there. I did 128.2 or something. I'd pushed and tried my hardest for no reward and I was wounded.

On lap two of the Senior race the following week I did 130.354. It just came to me when I got into a rhythm. The cheering, the atmosphere and the fact that we were all sucked into the 100th anniversary celebrations that year made it happen for me. When I did a 132mph lap years later, the buzz wasn't anywhere near as high as nailing that 130mph lap. Everybody was excited by it. I loved the fact that my Dad was there to see it. I wanted him to enjoy me racing on the Island as much as I used to enjoy watching him racing up in Jurby when I was a kid. Murray Walker, who has a huge connection with the TT, was also there., It was great to speak to him on that day.

It might sound a little bit cocky, but when I look back at the pictures of me drinking a pint, holding that 130mph sign, I can still hear the crowd shouting my name and I can see the look on people's faces as I was walking past them. Everybody was happy and I was chuffed to bits. I'm proud of a lot of the laps I've done round the TT course. My 250 record stood all the way through until 2016, when Bruce pipped it, but they all mean something to me. The lovely thing about that 130mph lap was that it was the only one that day. It would have devalued it if someone else had cracked 130mph as well. That day was a huge part of my journey.

*

I can still push myself. I did it in the Senior in 2015 and won it when nobody saw that coming. I served everyone that day and did what I reckon is one of the best TT laps I've ever done. It's funny what drives me to push nowadays. I remember winning in 2007 because I was fired up by a throwaway line from Guy Martin. He finished ahead of me at the North West that year and was giving it all his usual jibber jabber after the race. Plater, Guy and me were all battling for the win on the last lap. Plater came past me on the brakes, putting him in the lead ahead of me and Guy. Then Guy fucked himself up to pass me going into the Magherabuoy chicane, which let Plater off the hook and handed him the win. I ended up crossing the line in fourth place, which was frustrating. I still think we could both have had another go at Plater before the line if Guy hadn't gone into that chicane as hot as he did. Plater was a very determined rider and told me at Macau few years later that he'd have done whatever needed doing to win that day. I've never had that attitude.

Anyway, after the race, Guy said he was off back to work early the next morning and asked what all us factory boys were doing, going home to polish our big shiny motorhomes? It really upset me. He said that to me when he was 25. When I was that age I was laying bricks. I was up at six o'clock and out the door every day, scratching a living together so that I could go racing.

Guy had it miles easier than I did. I know he works on trucks, but I wasn't on fucking good bikes standing on the podium at 25. I was chucking bricks at a wall while I worried about how I'd find ten grand to pay Birdy to go racing and put food on the table at the same time. By 2007 I'd served my time. I'd earned the right to go home and polish my big shiny motorhome. It wasn't dropped down my chimney by Father Christmas.

Motorhomes aren't always about glamour. Mine is somewhere for my family to live when I'm racing because I don't want them sleeping in the back of a Transit van. I don't want them queuing up for a shower or a shit in the morning. Surely I've won enough races over the years to be able to have that without being made to feel like I'm showing off? Guy might have forgotten, or maybe he didn't know that I'd scratched my way to my first North West in '96 with just 90 quid to my name, or that me and Becky had lived in our motorhome a few years before because we didn't have a house.

Anyway, the point is that what Guy said to me at the North West pissed me off. It niggled at me and drove me to push that bit further to win next time we raced, which was at the TT. I did a 129.8mph circuit from a standing start on lap one, dominating early, just like Joey used to. Lap two was the big one, when I broke the 130mph barrier. I went on to win the race from Guy and Ian Hutchinson by over thirty seconds. I shook Guy's hand on the podium that day, looked him in the eye, gave his hand a little squeeze and told him I was off to polish my motorhome. That made me feel good.

I didn't mean it in a bad way. I'm not a bad person. Me and Guy haven't always seen eye to eye, off the track more than on it. But then we are very different people.

*

Later in 2007, I got a letter from the council informing me that they were giving me the freedom of the town, in honour of my contribution to motorbike racing and my continual promotion of Morecambe. We arranged a date for the presentation, I invited a few sponsors and took my family and the 130mph lap Fireblade along. It was a cool day, almost laughable really. Some guy came up with a big staff and clattered it against the door, shouting 'All rise!' We stood up and I had to swear under oath that I wouldn't deface Morecambe and all various other stuff. It was a bizarre tradition but a great thing to be a part of.

I was granted the right to drive sheep over the Skerton Bridge, which goes over the river Lune into Lancaster. I'm also allowed to graze my sheep on any piece of council-owned land in Morecambe, which would be handy if I had some sheep. I think I was probably the first person to be given the freedom of Morecambe who managed to get the Mayor on a Honda Fireblade for a picture. We had a good drink at the reception after the ceremony.

I'm very grateful that my home town has recognised what I do. I keep the scroll from the day safe with my TT trophies in the house. I'm proud of it. I suppose it begs the question why there has been no MBE, but like matching Joey Dunlop's wins at the TT, that's a question that everyone else assumes I'm interested in.

The thing with MBEs is that I find it hard to work out why people get them. If it's for contribution to a sport, I should have ten by now. Anybody who has an MBE gets my respect. David Knight has one, as does Carl Fogarty, and fair play to both of them. But why hasn't Neil Hodgson got one, or James Toseland or Chaz Davies? I don't know how it works but I know they don't pluck names out of a hat when they're dishing them out. Someone has to put you forward. Whether or not anyone has tried doing that on my behalf I don't know. But it would be a lovely touch to get one. Who wouldn't want the chance to go and see the Queen and get a pat on the back from her? She is the boss, end of.

I was awarded the Segrave Trophy at the Royal Automobile Club in 2015. It's given to those who display a 'Spirit of Adventure' on land, sea or air. In the past, it's been given to Lewis Hamilton, John Surtees OBE, Sir Jackie Stewart, Sir Stirling Moss, Colin McRae MBE, Barry Sheene MBE and a fair few other big names. It was

The American Eagle – loved it and loved travelling around Europe in it. Wanted to be Billy Big Balls in the paddock, so not many knew I didn't have a house to go home to.

Acting the goat at Macau, the year I took my only win in 2001. PR stunts are hard to take seriously when they involve dancing.

© NICK SOYE

When I'm at this stage, all eyes are on me. I can feel the weight of expectation on me, and all I want to do is get on with the job and go.

One lap, one rider and one 130.353mph ride into the record books. 2007, the centenary year at the TT. It's always great to cross the finish line at the Senior, but this one can never be repeated.

© CIARAN BROAD

Hand-painted, live results, thanks to local Scouts. Part of the tradition at the TT, but this was the first time anyone had to write 130 on it and it was mine.

Stood alongside Hutchy and the guy who is now my new teammate, Guy Martin. No better feeling in the world.

Getting the freedom of Morecambe and Lancaster in 2007. Being recognised by my community was a massive achievement for me.

Agostini failed to chat my mum up on the Island after she'd had a row with my dad. If she'd have jumped in his car, he could have been my dad and I could have been fast and good-looking. The man on the left actually is the daddy.

Murray Walker is a fantastic man to spend time with. Him taking time to talk to me and Ewan was a real privilege.

When Martin and Hutchy are spraying you with champagne, you know you've had a good day at the office.

Have that! Hutchy's strength of character is unbelievable; overcoming the odds like he has is nothing short of a miracle.

What goes up slows you down, fighting gravity on the AIM
Yamaha R1. People seem to forget about my time with Yamaha.
They were good to me and I delivered the goods for them.

Life on the road was ace in that motor home. Ewan used to love hanging about in the paddling pool. Here he is with Jim Moodie's grandson.

My son Ewan is 16 now, turning into a young man and making me proud every day. Back in 2004 I could still scoop him up for a kiss.

When it all gets a bit much, a quick nap on someone's shoulder is exactly what you need.

Having my family around me when I'm racing is massively important. Becky keeps my feet on the ground, no bother.

My daughter Maisie constantly amazes me. She's as bright as a button and as sharp as a knife. I love her to bits.

The best trophies in the world hug you back when you win.

The eyes tell the story here. Ride to live another day; job's a dream.

another proud day for me. Of course, it would be great to top that off with an MBE, as I've already mentioned. I've started telling people that I one already am one – a Motor Bike Expert. It's another one of the shit jokes I tell that make me laugh and Becky roll her eyes at me. I suppose it'll have to do for now.

If I was awarded one, I don't think I'd bother putting MBE after my name. Mervyn Whyte, who is the director of the North West 200, has an MBE, as does Gary Thompson, who is the clerk of the course at the TT. I suppose if somebody really wants me to have one, it'll happen. I do think it'd be great to meet the Queen. She is the daddy. I'd feel semi-wounded if it ended up being Prince Charles pinning it to my chest. It'd be nice for my kids too. I've served my sport well. I don't think Joey let his OBE go to his head, or that he thought in a million years that he would get one. But I do know that within his own four walls he'd have been dead proud of himself, and rightly so.

*

I was comfortable with the team set up that we had with Honda and expectations were high for 2008 because we had the new Fireblade, with backing from Padgett's. The single win that I had in the Senior race looks easy on paper because I finished 50-odd seconds ahead of everyone, but the reality is that it was tough. I battled with Bruce Anstey and Cameron Donald all the way. Bruce lost the lead in the first pit stop with a mechanical problem and Cameron's bike developed an oil leak on the last lap. I think the lead changed seven or eight times during the race. Cameron was on a flyer that year and won the Superstock and Superbike races. I didn't have much luck in the other races, grabbed a few podiums and had a DNF in both a 600 race and the Superbike race.

That win in the Senior meant I'd matched Mike Hailwood with 14 TT wins. It was a proud moment for me but it wasn't something I'd particularly set my sights on. I suppose it was around then that I started getting asked the big question that journalists and race fans have been asking me for years. I didn't think about surpassing Joey's record for TT race wins for a long time. I only think about it now because I get it driven into me. It's a story, a great headline. When people ask if I'm going for it, I think 'I might as well have a go at it'. Obviously when I first started racing the TT I dreamed about winning one, but if somebody had said back in '96 'here's your cards, you're going to win six' I'd have taken that deal. Wouldn't you? How the hell have I managed to win 23?

It wouldn't upset me if I didn't draw level with or surpass Joey's number of wins. As long as I do my best out there, I don't really care if I ever win another one or not. I've always said that. I love my pit mechanics and the people I work with to bits, I have huge respect for them, but the job they do isn't like the job I do. A bad day for them is a breakdown. A bad day for me means I'm done, I'm dead. I don't want to stick myself under that huge pressure of wanting to match Joey. It doesn't matter. As long as I'm hurtling round, riding well and enjoying myself, who knows what will happen? Joey didn't win a Superbike race between '88 and 2000. Twelve years without a win in that class is frightening. And he was 48 when he won in 2000. It was his time; it was meant to be.

Him having his accident in Estonia, was that meant to be? He was addicted and it felt like he wasn't ever going to stop. You can't just keep going and going and going with road racing. Destiny won't allow it. John Goodall couldn't give it up. He was 67 years old when he died following a crash out there. I'm not saying it's a bad thing and good luck to those that do carry on if that's what they choose to do. I think maybe Joey just didn't feel his age was a problem. Nothing could hold that family back.

The Dunlops are incredibly determined. Look at how defiant Robert was. I've seen him out there with a left thumb-operated front brake and a cheese grater wrapped around the throttle to stop it slipping through his gripless hands. He won the '98 125 TT race like that. Dogged little bastard. How much desire to win do you need? That family is amazing on that score. I can still picture Robert lying in the road at the North West in '98 after a crash, then walking onto the stage after he'd won and lobbing his crutches into the cheering crowd.

Joey died at 48 but he had 48 fantastic years and left an amazing legacy behind. He raised five great kids. Racing is selfish but he didn't do a bad job by his family.

*

Mark Webber came out for the TT in 2008 and we became good friends. It turns out he is a big-time TT fan. He was a big hitter in Formula One but he came to the TT with his dad with his civvies on and just wanted to be a bike fan. Mark had grown up ripping round the fields in Australia on dirt bikes and had always had a passion for two wheels. He came as a guest of Honda and was there when I won the Senior on the Padgett's bike. He came under the radar and I didn't know he was there until someone said he wanted to meet me.

We chatted about speedway, Lawson, Gardner and Mamola. Turns out Mark Webber is a big fan of that early 90s era of GP racing and really knew his stuff. He's pals with Mick Doohan and is up to speed with old two-stroke stuff. He could also sit and talk about triathlons and all sorts of weird sports. He seemed to have his finger on the pulse of most things.

He'd grown up similar to me in that he told all his mates he was off to be a racer and put all his money into the gamble, and they said they'd see him next week when it'd all gone tits up. He proved everybody wrong. We swapped details and stayed in touch. Most of our chat we share is about speedway racing. Fair play to anyone who can be as successful as him and still be a nice guy. I went to his 40th birthday, he's been back out to the TT and I've stayed at his house in Australia.

*

Back at home I was doing a great job of letting everyone know that, despite all those TT wins, I was far from superhuman. On one occasion, I was just about to take some bodywork up to my mate's place in my Volkswagen Transporter. It looked like it had been crashed into Halfords with body kit and bling hanging off it. I needed to get some stickers put on some bodywork and my mate was going to do it for me. It was freezing and had been snowing. I went out to warm up the Transporter for a bit before we set off and de-ice the screen. When I finished, I nipped in the house to say goodbye to Becky and have a quick wee. When I came out, the VW was gone. I shouldn't laugh, but I can now. I remember seeing this big black Transporter shape on the ground where the snow hadn't settled, and two lines leading away up the road. Somebody had hotwired it and driven off. I looked around expecting Jeremy Beadle to step out with a camera. He didn't. My van was gone.

Every time I've done something stupid like that and told Becky, she's had a tut and a bit of a snipe at me, but she's entitled to. I've probably lost more than five grand in cash over the years through being clumsy and forgetful. When I think back to how little we had when we first set out, I'm not surprised that she'd shout at me for being a knob with my stuff. I'll never learn though. I'm a nightmare, maybe a bit more like my dad than I think I am. But at the end of the day it's not hurting anyone.

CHAPTER 19

Ewan and Maisie

I'M UNDER NO illusions, women don't like me because I'm good-looking. They like me because I win TT races. Let's be honest if Wayne Rooney was driving a shovel in a quarry, the only person who would knock on his door would be the postman. I learned the hard way that the grass is definitely not greener on the other side. You think it is at the time, but it isn't. Through thick and thin, Becky has been there for me and we were able to pick up and rebuild what we had into something stronger than it was before. Having kids is a blessing and to me feels magical.

We'd discussed having more babies after Ewan was born and I knew that Becky would like another one. I was hesitant though, because I was still racing and there was always the danger that something could happen. Nine years after Ewan was born, Becky fell pregnant again. The circumstances were similar too. I had been fucking about and Becky and me had split up briefly again. When we got back together, I filled Becky full of arms and legs and little Maisie came along in 2010.

The birth was a difficult one, Becky insisted on having an epidural; she could obviously remember the pain of giving birth to Ewan. I was on my own in the hospital with Becky until a roomful of family turned up. Becky's mum, Steph, Becky's sister Ruth, my stepmum, Pam and a family friend called Karen, had all been on their way to a concert together but sacked it off and drove to the hospital instead. Them being there lightened the mood and they were all laughing and joking in the room while Becky was laying there.

Becky still laughs at me now about how when her dad, Dick made it to the hospital with Ewan, he arrived with a packed lunch for me because he knew that I'd be hungry. Becky was stretched out on the bed and I stank the place out eating a piece of ham off the bone in the chair next to her.

When Maisie eventually arrived, there was a lot less aggro than when Ewan was born, the epidural had clearly sorted the job out. Maisie was beautiful, I held her in my arms and danced around shouting, 'We got a pink one!'

Is there a right or a wrong way to have a family? I'm dead proud of the way we've raised our kids. They've had the opportunity to travel the world because of my job. Not many kids will get to see half of what ours have, and I like that. I've had people huffing and tutting at me because of our lifestyle, I've had bills from schools for taking them out of class to come racing with me, but in my eyes they're getting life experiences that they'd never get in a classroom in Morecambe.

Now that Ewan is a young man, we have a cracking relationship. He's my flesh and blood and I'll support whatever he decides to do when he's finished school 100 percent. He's been by my side from the day he shat his first nappy until the day you read these words and I would never change that. He's been through a bit as well – he has to deal with the fact that sometimes I take him to places and it feels like his dad is famous. He's been in the limelight too and he copes with it really well. If he steps out of line, his mother is there to rein him in but it's mostly me that gets the bollocking for treating him like a mate rather than a son. When Becky says that to me, I struggle to find the answer because he IS my mate.

I copped a right telling-off recently when she found out that I'd tried to get him into a nightclub. Ewan is still at school and I know we shouldn't have been doing that. When we were queuing up to get in, a lot of me wanted to go through with it and go in, but there was a voice nibbling away in my head telling me to slow down and remember his age (and reminding me what Becky would do if she found out). I knew we were on thin ice. In hindsight, I'm glad we didn't go through with it; he's only 15.

I'm waiting for him to ask me about the next steps when it comes to girlfriends. I think I'm ready to deal with that now. I was a late starter when it came to girls and pubs and so on. I was probably 17 before I went in a pub on my own and even then I didn't like it much.

I know that I couldn't have wished for a more pleasant and polite young man to call my son. I can take him into any kind of environment knowing I can leave him to speak to sponsors and so on without him being one of those cheeky little bastards you hear about. I know he's been under a bit of peer-pressure from his mates to drink and piss about, but he hasn't caved in. Well, I say he hasn't – you always want to believe what your kids tell you.

I sometimes scratch my head and wonder why Ewan isn't into bike racing. Becky thinks it's because he's surrounded by it and because I'm the opposite to my dad and haven't pushed him in that direction. I'm glad my dad did what he did, if he hadn't I wouldn't have everything that I have now, but I'm a completely different person. Ewan is calculated like me, probably even more so. He has the right temperament for racing but I don't want to pressurise him into anything he doesn't want to do. He's got a quad and he loves riding it, but we rarely get out on it for fear of me feeling like I'm pushing him. I don't mind taking my own risks but I don't want to make anyone else do something they don't want.

He's mint and Maisie is the same. I don't treat her any differently to how I treated Ewan when he was her age. She's a different kind of character, like a mini-Becky. Maisie constantly amazes me. She blows me away with her reading and how clever she is. I'm proud of them both. One of the most important things for me is that our children are surrounded by people who matter to them and care about them. I think they are. We're happy with things the way they are, but if a little swimmer made it all the way one day, I wouldn't be worried. I'd deal with it. Would I have another kid now? Yes, I think I would. We need to be mindful of the fact that I'm 44 and Becky is 41. Body clocks are ticking away here. But you can't shove them back in once they've arrived, can you?

*

On the one hand, I look at Valentino Rossi like a god and on the other, I think he's as normal as me and you. In a weird way, I see a bit of him in me and vice versa. He's ridiculously talented at what he does, but he's still a huge fan of the sport that he's been involved with for all these years. What a role model though, such a great guy to look up to.

The first time I spoke to him was at the TT in 2009. He wanted to experience it as a fan and did the lot, crammed into a hedge near Ago's leap watching us fly by. I think he was a bit in awe of the whole event. He rode a lap of the course when the roads were closed and enjoyed himself. He presented me with a trophy on the podium and the picture of us together helped me seal a deal with Monster Energy as one of their athletes.

I carried their logo on my helmet for the first time in 2009. I got in touch with them before the TT and said that I'd wear a Monster logo on my lid, and that if they didn't like what they saw, they wouldn't have to pay for it. But if they did like it, then maybe we could do a deal. I was investing in myself and it paid off because Rossi and me standing together on the podium was the money shot from that year's TT. He was already a Monster-sponsored athlete and I was wearing a Monster baseball cap. I've been with them ever since and we've signed a lifetime deal. Cheers Rossi, and big thumbs up! I didn't have that in my head as a plan and meeting him was special enough without thinking about deals and money.

Rossi is the greatest of all time, everyone is in awe of the man and his magic. I think there was definitely some mutual admiration and respect between us, which was great.

Later that year, Mark Webber arranged a private jet to go down to Valencia to watch the MotoGP. I'd never been in one before and was blown away by the experience. It was me, multiple speedway world champion Jason Crump and Adrian Newey, who was chief technical officer for the Red Bull F1 team. It was the year that Casey Stoner crashed the Ducati in practice, as well as being the year of the last ever 250GP race. Given my history with 250 two-strokes at the TT and being a British champion on one, it was great to be there for that.

I remember sitting about with Rossi, Mark Webber and Jason Crump feeling massively out of my depth. Looking back, I had no real reason to feel like that. I was definitely part of the gang that day, but in my head I was thinking, 'Jesus Christ, that's Rossi and Webber, sat next to Crump and the guy who designs Formula One cars for Red Bull. I'm just Jonnie Mac, the brickie from Morecambe. What the hell am I doing here?' It was good though, being accepted by company like that.

Rossi and I started chatting to each other through Twitter. Eventually we swapped numbers and he invited me out to his dirt-track ranch in his home town. Unfortunately, I've not had a chance to get out there yet because of my racing commitments, which is massively frustrating.

He has a 100km race there every year with a load of big-name racers, but it's usually on when I'm in Australia racing at the Island Classic. You'd think that you'd drop everything in a heartbeat to get out there if you were invited, but work is work and I end up putting that first. I'll get there though, one day. We still share text messages and weird pictures of stuff. He calls me McFuck. We have a good craic when we can.

The only way I can describe how it feels to have the greatest motorcycle racer of all time looking you in the eye on the TT podium with complete adulation is that it feels cool. It certainly greases your ego.

That man is entitled to every penny that he's worth, but every now and then I think about what he's earned and reckon that maybe I should have I've earned more than I have for doing what I've done. Apparently he's worth £110 million. Am I worth that? No, I am not! Like I said earlier, maybe if I'd have had a manager from the start I'd have a few more shillings in my pocket and wouldn't have cause to think like that.

Either way, to be able to call Valentino Rossi my mate is a very cool thing. I speak to Jorge Lorenzo on WhatsApp as well. The magic that those guys do makes them heroes to me. They consistently make it look easy. Guys like you and me can only ever imagine how it must feel to be able to do what they do on a motorcycle. They're finely honed guys who can perform day in and day out, while carrying enormous pressure on their shoulders. They go big, every single time. It's great that I've had the chance to be mates with them. It's good to know that if I was passing through, they'd stick the kettle on for me and vice versa.

It might not be as glamorous in Morecambe as it is in Tavullia, but I like the fact that Valentino still lives in the little town that he grew up in like I do. We could both be living it up in Monaco or somewhere but we choose to stay where our roots are. They still ring the bells in the local church every time he wins. As a nation, I think the Italians are more passionate about both life and racing than we are.

The pull that Morecambe has on me is weird. For my entire life, I've lived within six miles of the Queen Victoria hospital where I was born. Six houses and a motorhome, all within walking distance of each other. We've thought about moving to the Isle of Man and part of me would be really happy there. I've been asked me if I'd be able to put up with people knocking on my door or stopping me in the street all the time out there. I reckon I'd be fine. I know I'm popular and I don't think that's just because I've been successful on the bike. I think it's also because I don't mind having a bit of a craic with anyone who wants it. It's not like I'm Valentino Rossi and constantly get mithered. It's just 30 seconds here and there for people who ask for it. To be honest, I like the attention. People like having their egos greased, I don't care who they are. When someone stands next to you for a picture and tells you you're the bollocks, it feels nice. I like when it happens on the Isle of Man because I like Manx people, their way of life and their ethic. It's more laid-back than the rest of the UK. You could say they're shut off from the real world because the place is full of locals and not a lot else, but who's to say that they're not living a better life because they're cut off from normality a bit?

Half of me would go and live there tomorrow. Half of Becky would too, I think, but something has held us back. Maybe it's because we've only ever really lived in Morecambe. And at the end of the day, we're only three- and-a-half hours from Douglas anyway. By the time you've sat down in your front room for tea and watched a bit of a movie, we've jumped on a ferry and we're there.

I'm not sure if I lived there that I'd be up on the mountain doing 170mph everywhere just because I could. I think that would become dangerous after a bit. It's only now and then that you want to push your luck like that. The problem for me with that place is that it's always been a racetrack to me, and when I'm on it, I like to go fast. If I was going up the mountain and could see through to Guthries and knew there was nothing coming, wallop, I'd be racing, whether I was on the school run or off for a bag of chips.

It makes me wonder how you distinguish between what's dangerous driving for someone who does what I do for a living and someone else who doesn't. If you showed a video of me riding over the Mountain at the Isle of Man to 100 people, 99 of them would thing it was dangerous. But it's isn't to me. When the roads are open to the public, I've seen people ride along that same stretch at half the speed I do it at, and they're so far out of their depth it has to be classed as reckless driving. Where do you draw the line? Who gets done and who gets let off?

*

2009 was Honda's 50th year of racing and they expected big things at the TT. I delivered exactly that in the Superbike race, winning my 15th TT and claiming the outright lap record along the way. Steve Plater and Guy Martin shared the podium with me, both on Hondas, and Hutchy and Gary Johnson finished fourth and fifth. That gave Honda the top five positions in the race. I also bagged fifths in the Superstock and one of the Supersport races. I was leading the Senior and it looked like I was on for a win until my chain snapped on lap four. I was gutted, all that work and effort, only to end up watching the end of the race from the side of the road. Macau ended the same way for me that year, but I did manage a win in the British Superstock championship at Croft.

CHAPTER 20

Lied to Becky

RIDING DIFFERENT CATEGORIES of bikes at the TT satisfies me in different ways. On the Superbike, I feel I've done something unbelievably challenging. There are times I've lost time on a Superbike because I've just been a passenger. You are the boss of a 600 but sometimes a Superbike is boss of you. I don't care who you are or what you've achieved at the TT, you just have to accept that you're not making all the decisions on the big bikes and you're on top of a 180mph projectile that's out of your hands at times.

It's taken a long time for people to suss out the Superbike class. I was able to get away with it for years, having the confidence to nip off at the start and put in hot first and second laps. It takes stacks of experience to know just how hard you can push when the bike is full of fuel and the tyres aren't ready, but that's what you have to do if you want to win races at the TT. Then follow that up with a really slick pit stop, bang, job done. By this time the rest of the field can be 25 seconds behind you. I've been on the receiving end. I've seen my board telling me I'm 30 seconds behind the leader and there's almost nothing you can do to close that gap.

It's difficult to understand that you're off line when you're only a few inches from where you should be on a section. You just have to take it on the chin, ease off slightly and sacrifice a bit of time to sort yourself out. You can't think that you can immediately pull the thing to where it needs to be because you can't. Every corner is linked and each section has to flow from one to the next. It's the kind of thing that's hard to teach racers who are new to the place. You need to keep putting the laps in until you get a feeling for where you need to be everywhere on the track to maximise your speed. You have to feed the bike into every corner and sometimes the right line in one section comes from being at the right point on the track four corners before.

On the Superbike, it's a constant fight with the bike and the road. Getting these things right comes from good preparation. Making the most of practice, making sure you're relaxed enough at the start to control your breathing all the way round, even keeping an eye out for wind direction changes that can have an effect on where you need the bike to be. You have to get out there to learn all that stuff. You can sit in a classroom and talk about it all day, but until you get out on the road and start making small mistakes, you don't learn how to deal with the frustration and anger that you'll feel when you get something wrong. It's hard to get anywhere near a perfect lap. If you string all the best times through all the sectors together, the best lap possible at the minute is 135mph. I've still never come close. When I took the lap record at 132.7mph in 2015, I was only the fastest in one sector.

I'm pretty sure Steve Plater still holds the fastest time from the Ramsey Hairpin to the Bungalow, and that was in 2009. You cannot fault that man's determination, but I think ultimately it finished him off when he crashed at the North West in 2010. Luckily he got away with it. I was in the debrief before him and he was on pole from the Tuesday night. The weather was looking bad for the Thursday but he wanted to go even quicker than he had done to get pole.

I told him he was mental and asked him what he thought he was going to prove when he was already on pole. What did he do next time we were on the bikes? He came steaming past me and then went through a hedge backwards. That mindset pissed me off a bit really. This is road racing, you can't approach it like a short circuit. I could write ten books about other people, but I don't want to be rude about them and that isn't the intention here. Steve is a good guy and we get on well. I suppose some people just approach road racing differently from me. I just don't like seeing anyone get injured. If all the planets are aligned and I'm flat out going for a win and make a mistake, I can take that on the chin, but you have to ride to the conditions. You match your pace to them, not the other way round.

I got a bit of a slagging off for making noises about a few things when it's come to road racing in the wet. I'm well within my rights to do that and I don't care what anybody else says. It hurts a little bit because I'm a man and we think we have to be tough guys, but I've ended up being one of the racers that organisers speak to when the conditions are questionable. I give my opinion based on my experience and sometimes that involves having to say it's too dangerous. But there'll always be someone else who is willing to get out there and have a go, which is fine. They can crack on. It's hard to say you don't think you should race when you have the pressure of a team and an expectant crowd out there but conditions have to be right for the riders.

I did a wet race at the TT in 1998 when I was young and daft and didn't care. I nearly fell off ten times. I finished third behind Joey Dunlop and Bob Jackson. I earned about 1500 quid, for nearly killing myself multiple times. I said after that day that I wouldn't ever do that kind of thing again and I haven't. I'll go out in the wet and do what I'm obligated to do for my sponsors and my team, but when it's wet, getting back in one piece is the number one priority for me and that's it. I will have already told them before we signed a deal together. That might sound a bit too negative, like I've given up when I haven't, but being a TT racer doesn't mean I'm stupid.

*

Becky's dad died in 2010. It was horrendous. I loved the guy to bits. He did so much for me – welcomed me into his house, allowed me to date his daughter, gave me a job when I needed money and shared his coffee with me when I was cold. I felt like his son, I respected and trusted him. He didn't need to allow me into his life but he did.

I was testing my race bike at Bruntingthorpe the day he died, doing high-speed stability tests with Dunlop. Becky didn't want me to go because she knew that Dick was close to dying and wanted me to be there. Like a knob, I went to do the test, telling her everything would be fine. I was going up and down the airfield as fast as I could but in the back of my mind were Becky and her dad, who was at death's door.

Throughout the day I was checking in with Becky on my mobile, and every time I did, she'd tell me to come home to be with them. I kept saying that I'd get away as soon as I could. The thing that kicks me right in the guts is that Becky rang me and I told her that I was in the van and would be there soon. I put the phone down, did up my leathers and got back on the bike for one last run. While I was riding down the bloody runway, Becky rang again and Neil Tuxworth answered my phone. He told her that I was out doing my last test run of the day, after I'd lied to her and told her that I was already on my way home.

When I pulled in and Neil told me that he'd taken a call from Becky I felt hideous. Everybody else from the family was there apart from me. After being with me for all this time, I think Becky semi-understood why I was doing what I was doing. But that didn't make the fact that he died while I was riding up and down an airfield, being a selfish prick, any easier to get my head around. Like missing Joey's funeral to race that wildcard in the World Championships, if I could turn back the clocks and put people ahead of motorbikes, I would do it for Dick Langley in a heartbeat. I still miss him.

*

My results at the 2010 TT were pretty shit to be honest. I had a fourth in the Superstock race and a fifth in one of the Supersport races. Some years are better than others and 2010 was just one to chalk up to experience and move on from. I only managed a sixth at Macau but I did have a win and a podium in the two superbike races at the North West. It hasn't all been podiums and piss ups. I always give my best on the bikes, but sometimes the results just aren't there. I've finished 18th on production Triumphs and wondered where the hell was going wrong.

In the 2011 Senior race, Guy Martin was 11 seconds ahead of me at one point on the Relentless Suzuki. I managed to close that gap on him. I pegged him back here and there, took a few seconds out of him in the pits, and I beat him. The first person to come and congratulate me was Guy. I've got a great picture on the wall of my garage of the moment he came over and gave me a cuddle. He leaned in, whispered into my ear and told me I was a hero. It meant a lot to me.

That year, I won one of the Superbike races by almost a minute from Cameron Donald and Gary Johnson. I also came second in the Superstock race as well as one of the other Supersports. We had a bit of a laugh in the press conference after that one. It was my 50th TT finish and the 32nd time I'd made the podium. When I got my chance to speak, I let everyone know that my foreskin had rolled back on lap one and I'd basically spent an hour and a bit chafing the end of my lad. It got a laugh in the room and definitely got my sponsors some good coverage. The video of the interview ended up on websites all over the world.

*

In 2011 I was back at Le Mans for first time since 2004, when I rode in the Honda TT Legends road race endurance team. Me, Steve Plater, Cameron Donald and Keith Amor did well in our first meeting – we bagged a fifth at the Bol d'Or at Magny-Cours.

Russell Benney ran the team. He had stacks of experience. The pit crew has to be perfectly drilled in everything from changing a back wheel to rebuilding a smashed-up bike at one in the morning. Russell had the chops to do that and when we finished fifth in that first race, everybody thought we were great. The media seemed to love the fact that we were all from a road racing background and everyone got behind the team. Endurance racing seems to be a national pastime in France and they totally got into what we were doing.

We got right into the thick of it, bagging a fourth at Oschersleben. We were laying in fourth at Albacete as well until I crashed on my in-lap. It was my last stint on the bike and was going well until a pipe blew off the water pump and spat me off.

I enjoyed riding in that team and liked the different buzz that endurance racing gave me. We did okay at Qatar at the end of the season as well, with another fourth. We ran a three-man team there. Cameron had fallen down some stairs at home and couldn't ride, so we got on the phone to Glen Richards and had him out as the third rider with me and Keith, who had a collarbone pointing the wrong way at the time.

Me and Glen ended up doing back-to-back stints for most of that race, which involved full hours in the blistering heat of the day, then into the night under floodlights.

We stayed out there for a few days before the race and every day we'd drive out of downtown Doha to the circuit in Losail in this poor little Nissan rental car. It was hired on a credit card from my wallet but we all took turns to beat the shit out of the thing.

We had a journalist called John Hogan hanging out with us the whole time we were there. He was the editor from SuperBike magazine and we all seemed to hit it off. He's the guy who helped me put this book together. We've worked on a couple of projects over the years and we get on well. We spoke about doing a book while we were on the Qatar trip. I'd already done plenty in my career but it feels like there's more juice to talk about now that we've waited a few years. I've won another five TTs for a start.

We ended up dressed in full Arab kit one night, three riders and a journalist, cruising downtown Doha in this poor Nissan that had been bounced off every kerb in town and blending in with the crowd. God knows where the idea came from to dress like locals, but we ended being fitted out in a little shop in the market square. We asked if anyone would be offended and they just laughed at us, so we cracked on.

We had late-night coffee and a puff on a shisha pipe with the locals, then went and watched a local band and had some fun. I like doing that kind of thing, seeing a bit of the world. A lot of racers would spend their evenings in their hotel room watching porn on an iPad. The way I look at it, I might never get the opportunity to go back to these places again, so I want to collect a few memories and have a laugh. I've done lots of races that are easy to forget but I'll always remember that meeting because of the fun we had that night. We blended in so well that when we got back to the hotel, we took a table opposite Neil Tuxworth (the team boss) in the restaurant, thinking he'd clock us straight away. Twenty minutes later, Neil was still tucking into his dinner completely unaware that it was us lot sat a couple of metres away.

I was on a tight schedule, so after the race we grabbed a quick beer and then Keith and the boys dropped me at the airport. I jetted off to Macau and thought nothing more of the trip, until about six months later when I started getting speeding fines in the post from the car hire company. It turned out that once they'd dropped me off, the boys rallied the fuck out of Nissan past as many speed cameras as they could find. It was worth it, I enjoyed myself out there. A cracking result for the team and a good laugh with the lads.

I've done a bit of endurance racing since the TT Legends stuff but not on as big a scale. Maybe we're not French enough for proper endurance racing. Those boys love it and their riders are like machines, they just go and go. No disrespect to anyone who does endurance racing, but it did sometimes feel like a bit of a holiday for most of the grid, with a few really sharp boys going fast at the front. Most bike fans will have probably never heard of guys like Vincent Philippe and Anthony Delhalle, but last year those boys were properly rapid and at the top of their game. Riders like them often don't get the credit they deserve. For some reason they don't shine when you take them out of that French endurance racing environment, but when you're in their backyard you know about it. Sadly, Delhalle was killed as I was finishing this book.

*

Sometimes I meet people who don't know me and don't know much about road racing, but they've seen on-board footage of me at the TT and they tell me I must be completely mad. Everybody is entitled to their opinion and I know that from the outside the way we ride the roads must look insane but I do sometimes get a bit pissed off with people when they say that. Because I'm polite, I can laugh it off, but half of me wants to say, 'Fuck you, I'm not mad, I'm a sportsman, this is my job, which I take very professionally and by the way I am quite talented. There is an element of skill in what we do. We're not just fucking lunatics'.

It's not easy to do thousands of laps round that place, only to be told by someone who doesn't get it that you're an idiot. I wouldn't dream of saying that, but it's difficult to get the message across to the man in the street sometimes. I don't give a fuck who you are or what you've done. If you don't enjoy watching bikes at the TT, you're not alive and there's something wrong with you. If you stand at the side of the road when a bike goes past you absolutely flat-out and you don't get wrapped up in the atmosphere, then you, my friend, are fucked. It's so different, so unique, fast and intense. You couldn't do it if you were mad. Anything can happen and things can go wrong in a split second, but we're risk-takers and those happen to be the risks we're willing to take.

I once did a thing called 'Chimp Management'. An English sports psychiatrist called Dr Steve Peters developed the idea. It's a scientific study of the how the human brain processes information, including risk. Apparently, there are three parts to our brains. The human part, which is at the front of the brain, deals with facts and known truths in order to make logical decisions. Then there's the chimp part, which isn't strictly under your control. It deals with feelings and emotions and puts information together based on those things. Then there's the computer part, which stores data provided by the other two parts. This data forms our memories and can provide us with stored information if the chimp or human parts of our brains don't come up with what we need quickly enough, or if we choose to let the computing part of our brain provide the answers based on its previous decisions.

After the study, they told me that my brain could calculate risk and make decisions far quicker than the average human's. When some people are driving down the road using their mobile phones, it can feel like everything has sped up because they're asking their brains to process driving at the same time as having a conversation. When I do it, I feel like I could make a sandwich at the same time. The information is coming in through my eyes and my processor is telling me that everything is okay, in fact that it's better than okay, it's safe and easy and I can take on more information. That extra information could involve making a sandwich, or it could involve accelerating to 190mph. It's not my fault that some people can overload their brains if they creep over the 30mph limit on the way home from work. I see it when I give people pillion rides. I'm not trying to talk myself up, but some of them shit their pants. It's simply because their brains aren't calibrated in the same way as mine.

The downside to the way my brain works is that my attention span is limited, as I mentioned before. Once you've locked me into something, I'll give it everything in terms of effort and attention, but if I'm not interested I'm off doing something else within minutes. When you do what I do for a living, that isn't such a bad way to be. My inner chimp helped me to win the Superbike and Superstock races in 2012. I also had my first ride on the Mugen Shinden electric bike, finishing second in a field of only four. I came home a 19-times Isle of Man TT winner.

CHAPTER 21

A Bag Full of Sandwiches

WHEN I BEAT Michael Dunlop by ten seconds in the Senior in 2013, he did the same thing that Guy had done after the 2011 Senior race. He was the first person to come and congratulate me. I like to see the best in others. Lots of people think he's prickly and hard to get on with but I really like him. I like Conor Cummins too, they're great lads. They're not afraid to speak their minds and rock the boat a bit if they need to, though.

Conor has become a really good friend of mine. Along with trusting him and knowing that we can race wheel-to-wheel at silly speeds, I like that our missuses are close friends. My daughter Maisie is going to be a bridesmaid at his wedding and I like being friends with him. I know a lot of racers who don't want to become too friendly with anyone for a different reason, which is that they want to beat everyone. So do I, but I like being friends with nice people.

Michael had won four races on the bounce and it looked like he was going to win all five. The 600 lap record he set that year still stands now. It was phenomenal but it's dropped off everyone's radar because it was on a 600. He did a 131mph lap on a Superstock Fireblade: un-fucking-real. He was on fire and it looked like a foregone conclusion that he was going to win the Senior and make it five. But I had different thoughts.

At the start of the race I was feeling the pressure more than usual. That year I'd worn Joey Dunlop replica leathers and helmet in the Superbike race, on a bike that was painted in Joey's Honda colours. I think I maybe spent too much time trying do the Joey Dunlop story justice rather than the John McGuinness story. I ended up getting a lazy start in the Senior but I won that six-lap race hands down and felt proud to have done so.

Michael and I were on identical machinery that year, prepared in the same way, so there wasn't a lot he or anyone else could say after I won. That he was the first man to come and congratulate me was very special to me, not least because I don't want the other lads to think I'm a dick. The thought that they might hurts me. I don't think that of them and I've always tried to be a fair rider who wants to see them succeed. When I'm beaten, I'm the first person to shake them by the hand. If they win, they deserve it. But I've been in their shoes as well. I was a young gobshite once, like when I put that pass that was too close on Joey and learned a lesson big time. I grew up in a breath when he destroyed me in the 250 race that followed.

Now everyone is sharp. They're fast in practice and they're putting the work in, especially in the early laps. I've been doing that under the radar and have nibbled out six or seven wins riding like they all are now. With the greatest of respect to everyone I wasn't going to tell anyone how I was doing what I was doing. I just had that confidence to push hard from the off.

*

Fighting isn't my thing, never has been. I did end up giving a guy a slap on the Isle of Man in 2013 though. I didn't see it coming until it was right under my nose. I'd taken Becky and the kids across to go to the Joey Dunlop Foundation dinner. It was a freezing cold January and we'd taken the night ferry from Heysham, which meant we arrived in Douglas at about six in the morning. It was pitch black and cold, and I had a half-snoozing Maisie in my arms when we were checking into the Empress hotel on the promenade. I was still half asleep myself as I lugged the suitcase in from the boot of the car. Some nosher followed me into the lobby and started yapping at me. He'd dumped his pushbike outside and was going at it, clearly on something which I don't think was drink. 'Who the fuck do you think you are, coming over here and doing this?' he slurred at me. He didn't have a clue who I was, not a jar of glue.

Once I'd worked out that it wasn't a joke, I just asked the guy behind reception to give me my keys so I could get Becky and the kids out of the way and up to our room. The young lad was dithering and flapping, trying to get me to sign all kinds of paperwork. I just said, 'Let me get the kids up to the room and I'll be straight back down to sign and sort everything.' I thought this would give the lad who had been shouting his mouth off a chance to bugger off.

Meanwhile, he's behind me, calling me a wanker and laughing at me for nothing. I reached the end of my tether and called the guy a prick, told him to shut up and demanded the key to our room from the poor lad behind the counter. I turned to have another yip at the dickhead and Becky told me not to bother as it wasn't worth the aggro. She was right (again) so I turned my back on him. He laughed at me again. 'Ha, you wanker, go and hide behind your stupid bitch of a wife,' was what he said next.

My head went, so I turned round and let him have one. Anyone that knows me will say that I'm not a fighter, but I punched him from the ends of my toes up and he went down like a sack of shit. I started panicking then, thinking I'd killed the guy, so I went to grab the keys so we could get out of the way. The next thing I knew, the guy was up off the floor with his fists in the air. 'I wasn't ready, try that again!' he said. So we went at it again.

It wasn't nice in front of the kids, but I wanted him out, so I grabbed him by the hood of his jumper and posted him out of the door of the hotel. All the while he's shouting the odds about checking the CCTV cameras and having me done for assault.

By now, someone at reception had called the police, who arrived minutes after it had all calmed down. They said they'd been tracking the guy on CCTV and had seen him trying car-door handles in town. The guy had a ladies' scarf in his pocket that he'd lifted from someone's glovebox and had clearly been pissing around all night before we bumped into him.

One of the coppers was a racing fan and seemed quite excited to be talking to me. I apologised to him and said that I had no other option but to defend my family because the guy wouldn't leave us alone. As I was explaining myself, his radio crackled into life. It was the superintendent or someone, asking for an update on the situation. The copper said, 'We've got John McGuinness here, some guy has been abusive towards him and his family.' The chief at the other end said, 'Has he hit him?' When the copper in front of me said that I had, there was a pause and then a short sharp response from the radio: 'Good. Good lad!'

I had to go down the station and make a statement later but I didn't mind because I didn't think I'd done anything wrong. It was still quite scary though. Until then I'd never been in the back of a police car, heading for the station to talk about a scrap I've had. Obviously I've been in a few scuffles over the years like most people, but nothing that involved statements and the law. The police out there had been trying to nail this guy for a while and I think he got a couple of weeks in jail out there. Those boys on the island don't mess about.

I may never have been in the back of a police car before, but I was pulled over once out there for driving without a seat belt on. There were four of us in the car and we'd gone round the Ramsey hairpin and started climbing the mountain when they stopped me. Bearing in mind there's no speed limit up there, I asked the copper if we needed seat belts to just keep us in one handy bag if we ended up going off the mountain upside down at 150mph. We had an argument that turned into us having a bit of a laugh. He wanted to give everyone in the car a ticket each. I was trying to get him to give us one between the lot of us. As much as I was being funny with him, I don't argue with the police and I respect the job they do. We bartered our way down to two tickets. I took them on the chin and off we went.

They did me for texting on my paddock scooter as well. Again, I was in the wrong and there was no defence from me.

Anyone who's ever been stopped by the police on the Isle of Man will know that they have a big job to do managing everyone when the TT is on. It can't be easy. They deserve some respect and they get it from me, especially if I'm in the wrong, which I usually am. They seem to apply a bit more of a common sense approach to policing than elsewhere. If you've got a black visor on in the daytime, they'll wave you past. If you've got one on in the middle of the night, you deserve to have your bollocks felt. Same goes for two-inch number plates and all the other crap we've all tried to get away with over the years.

At the end of the day if you're riding with a noisy pipe, most people only hear you for a few seconds and then you're gone. It shouldn't really matter unless you're banging up and down the prom in first gear pissing everyone off. On the flipside, if you steal stuff or get caught with drugs, they will absolutely nail your hat on, and in my mind there is nothing wrong with that at all. That seems to be how they look at things on the Isle of Man and I like that.

*

Eleven weeks before the TT in 2014, I crashed my enduro bike into the hardest rock in the universe. I broke my wrist, did a few ribs and busted myself up really badly. I thought I might have to miss the TT that year but got stuck into physio and hoped that I'd be all right. I look back now at and realise that I probably shouldn't have been riding the Superbike. I'm being hypocritical though – I know as well as anyone how much the TT draws you in. I opted to pull out of one of the 600 races, to recharge and give myself a better a chance on the big bike, and I got away with it. I spoke to Clive Padgett and said I needed to have a rest. Even if I didn't have a single penny to my name, I wouldn't have ridden the bike because I didn't want to put myself or anyone else in any danger. That was the first time I've ever done that. That year I rode some of the worst TT laps I've ever done. The only time I got anywhere near the podium was when I was walking through the paddock.

Because of the injury my confidence was low. I felt bad for Clive, he'd put me on good bikes and I just couldn't ride them to the best of my ability. I knew he was disappointed, which just made me feel worse. I love Clive to bits, he's like family to me and I didn't like the fact that there was tension between us. Having to tell him that I was going to sit out a 600 race so that I could ride in the Senior was really tough. The team had put in hours of effort and bike prep time, and all the costs that come with that. But I suppose that if that's one of the lowest points of my career, I'm doing all right, and I don't want to sound like I'm whinging.

Clive respected my decision and said that he agreed with it but we were at each other a bit before the Senior.

He said something to me after one of the pre-race presentations that really narked at me. I could understand why he was feeling like that though and when he threw a wobbler at me I took it on the chin and walked away. I'd made a comment about a handlebar coming loose and Clive let me have it with both barrels. There's a perfectly good reason why Padgett's have been in business for nigh on 60 years and that's because they prepare some of the best race bikes in the world. I've always thought that and I think Clive thought I was having a snipe at the quality of his work. I wasn't.

It didn't take long for us to get over it and we've been the best of mates ever since. I hate confrontation. I hate the idea of saying something that I'll regret later on, even though in this case I had nothing to say because it was my fault I couldn't ride.

Making that decision was a tough one, but nowhere near as tough as having to get my head around what happens if you ignore what your body is telling you. Simon Andrews' death hit me hard. I thought he was a bit of a dick when I first met him, a bit of a gobshite and over-confident. But he wasn't like that at all. He was a lovely lad, funny, witty, quirky and different. He also adored my kids, and anybody who comes into my life and has time for my children will always be welcomed by me. Just like DJ, Simon was like a kid himself. I had masses of respect for Simon when he battled his way back from injury. The determination he showed was amazing. His unstoppable 'wanna race' attitude was unquestionable, but I do ask myself why he was even in the NW200 in 2014. I remember him saying to me, 'If I finish eighth in this race, I can pay for some physio.' What the fuck! I asked him how much he wanted and offered to pay for his treatment. I told him there'd have been another time, another race and another opportunity for him to achieve his goals.

He was only 31 when he was killed at the North West 2014. The worst part for me was questioning whether he made a mistake, or if he wasn't strong enough to be on the bike. I don't think he was 100 percent fit and I reckon no one should be road racing unless they are. I mean, in hindsight, I'd probably have had a better TT in 2014 if I'd taken a carrier bag full of sandwiches and a few beers and sat in the crowd with everyone else.

*

I'm so clumsy with some things. I get blasé about stuff now and then and it catches me out. Some things I cherish and don't want to let out of my sight, others I just seem to forget to care about. Like the time in 2014 I had my watch stolen out of my van. I forget to lock my cars and trucks up a lot of the time and left a Graham watch that had been presented to me on the podium for winning a Senior TT. It's worth about ten grand. I came out to my van one morning and the bloody thing was unlocked. Someone had been in it. The door was ajar, and there was no sign of my trials helmet, sat nav or the watch. Oh dear. This was a limited edition. There were only ten in the world and I had number seven.

I went to the police station to report it. I showed them a picture and asked them if someone had handed it in. They had no idea what they were looking at or its value. When I told them it was worth ten grand their ears pricked up. They posted on their Twitter and Facebook pages. It went nuts. Within a few hours, the posts had been shared right across the country. The police got an anonymous phone call from somebody saying they had my watch. I didn't want to know who had it or who'd been in my truck, I just wanted it back. We'd made that watch too hot to handle and whoever had it realised they couldn't do anything with it. I don't know how the mind of a thief works, but they had the choice of smashing it to bits and lobbing it in the sea, or just handing it back. Luckily for me they chose option two.

I got the watch and my sat nav back, but not my trials helmet and that pissed me off. It was a cool custom-painted Shoei and I was gutted. It was my fault and I should have locked my van, but a vehicle being unlocked doesn't give someone else the right to go in and help themselves. It's my stuff in my fucking van.

I had an MX lid pinched from my van another time and saw a young lad riding down the street on a scooter with it on a few months later. I flashed him and pulled him over. I didn't go steaming it and attacking him, I just asked him where he got it. He was flapping and didn't have any answers. I told him it was mine and that I was taking it home. He told me he'd given 20 quid for it in a pub. The kid was all right, he said he didn't know it was mine. I offered to give him his twenty quid back and call it quits, so I got it back.

I almost lost that watch again a year or so after I got it back. I put it in one of the trays at Manchester Airport Security and forgot to pick it up on the other side of the X-ray machine. I wandered off into the shops and was looking at bike magazines when the tannoy went off. 'Ding dong, has anybody left a watch at security?' I went running back over and there were a couple of guys waiting to talk to me. They had no idea of the value. When I took it back I decided it was time to stop wearing it every day. I appreciate the watch that Graham presented me with, the build quality is amazing, but they just don't do much for me. I'm just too clumsy with stuff like that.

CHAPTER 22

The Tap on My Shoulder

THE 2015 TT looked like it was going to be a repeat performance of the year before. The pace at the front of every race was massive and they all seemed full of potential winners. I won the Zero TT on the Mugen bike and it looked like that would be all she wrote for me that year, until the day of the Senior.

I was up for it the moment my eyes opened on race day. I got off to a good start but the race was red flagged when Jamie Hamilton crashed. The restart time was announced and I had to go through the process of getting ready all over again. Hutchy had been leading before the red flag but I still felt like I could win. When the race restarted, I managed a 131mph lap from a standing start. The weather and road conditions were just perfect and I was on one from the word go. On lap two, I did a 132.701mph lap, my fastest ever. I spent the whole of the next lap being cheered by what felt like everyone on the island. It was an incredible feeling, crossing the line knowing that I'd set a lap record, as well as serving everyone who thought that I was done for the week. I was a 23-times TT winner. This was an unbelievable achievement and we celebrated massively afterwards. I'd proved that I still had what it takes to do the job round there.

The celebrations started almost immediately, back in the Honda hospitality unit. It didn't all go quite to plan though. I met Carol Vorderman while I was still in my leathers. Keith Amor was running the hospitality as he wasn't riding and I was in there giving a speech and doing a meet and greet. I had a bit of a chat with her and thought she was a tidy old thing. When we'd finished chatting to her I went over to Keith who was talking to a group of people. I slid into the conversation and said something like, 'Fucking hell, she's still a tidy old thing is that Carol Vorderman, I'd definitely throw one up it.' Keith started glaring at me, not saying anything but willing me to stop talking about her. I was oblivious to his signs and asked Keith if he'd give her one, again commenting on how tidy she was for an old bird.

Keith turned to me and said 'John, let me introduce Graham, he's Carol's boyfriend.' Graham was a big bastard and for a split second he looked like he was going to murder me, then he just smiled and said he'd heard it all before and not to worry about it. A few weeks later I bumped into her again in a hospitality suite at Silverstone. I asked her if she'd enjoyed her time at the TT and she smiled and said yes. She didn't know me from a bar of soap and clearly had no idea that we'd met just a few weeks before. She disappeared into the room and that was that. I didn't lose any sleep over it but I'd still chuck one up her.

*

Every year for the last few years, I've made sure to ride the superbike I'm going to race the next day last thing the night before. Every bike I race feels different from the rest so I'll take the big one to Douglas Head, scrub my tyres in and sit on the bike. I'll run up and down a little private road a few times, getting a feel for the bike. Then I can go back to the motorhome and sleep on how it felt.

People think I'm mad for scrubbing tyres and don't think it'll make any difference, but it does to me. It can determine whether you fall off at Quarterbridge or not, which I did on the Paton in the Classic in 2016. All that experience, all those years of telling everyone else to tiptoe through on cold tyres, and there I was, on my head. I had the ultimate amateur crash. I was so pleased that after 20 years of racing the TT, that was the corner that I crashed on. The law of averages dictates the if you ride that place as much as I have, eventually you will fall off somewhere. If I had to choose anywhere on the whole lap to fall off, it'd be there. Another TT box ticked, if you like. I've never told anyone this before, but I nearly lost the front on the electric bike last year as well. It was during practice and I was up at Brandywell. That scared me. I tried to go into it deeper and quicker than I normally would.

The electric bikes are too quick now to only do two laps in practice and then race. It's not enough time to get your brain to understand the bike. I know the limits on all the other bikes I ride, but I still don't on the electric one. Superbike laps are consistent. You ride round until you need more fuel, then you carry on as before. I might do one lap on the electric bike running 80 kilowatts of power, then the team downloads the data and it tells them that the next lap needs 85 kilowatts, so the job changes completely. And I've had a new bike every year so there's no consistency yet because of constant development.

All that plus the fact that it can be massively different from one lap to the next means it's hard to find the limit. What I really want to do is whang one of them up the road on a short circuit in order to find the limit, but obviously I can't do that. These things are made of unobtanium, it's not like I could rob a peg from the car park for one like we used to have to with the KR1.

Because of that, when I pushed a bit deeper into Brandywell than normal, the bike tried to bite me. It wasn't like I tucked the front – the thing weighs 260 kilos. I think I folded the front tyre a bit on the rim. It just couldn't take what I was asking of it. It was a weird feeling, unlike anything I'd had before. It was as if the bars were turned but the tyre had carried on in a straight line. This told me that maybe the yokes aren't strong enough for the bike.

It's funny how some people have reacted to the electric bike, moaning and saying that it's not a proper TT machine. I tell you what, a massive amount of work goes into that bike. The Zero race is a real heads-or-tails moment for me. Am I going to win or not? It's a question of working out how much I'm willing to push into the unknown on the thing. To do 119.8mph on a quarter of a ton of electric bike is not hanging about. The corner speeds are incredible and they're only going to get quicker. And the bikes will get lighter.

*

Those last ten minutes before the start of a race are the worst. Somebody might come up to me with a pint of beer in his hand when there are two minutes to go and ask me to sign his hat. I can feel myself screaming inside, wondering if this guy has any idea what it feels like to be standing in my boots. But, of course, he doesn't. That's one of the reasons why I never rev at people when they approach me. I can't complain about somebody coming up to me to say good luck or asking me to sign something. So I just smile back and say thanks very much to them. The easiest thing would be to tell them to go and get fucked but they're fans and they're on a big jolly.

Becky puts the coin down my leathers just before I go. She's the last person I speak to. I give her a little kiss, stick my lid on and I'm away. The man who taps me on the shoulder is the last person to touch me, but it's Becky who I speak to last. By the time it gets to that stage, everything feels a bit surreal. If the fittest bird in the world were to come up to me and flash her tits, it wouldn't register.

I like to look up at the grandstand to see if I can spot the kids before I go, to have one last look at Becky, Maisie and Ewan so I can drink a bit of them in and take it away with me down the road. I'm hoping that I'll see them all again.

In the last few seconds before I pull away, I shut out the world and I'm ready to race. It's a funny situation to be in and one that not many will ever understand. All eyes are on you, the fans are staring from the side of the road, the helicopter is beaming a shot of you all over the world and your name is crackling over the radio. It feels like things are a little bit out of your control. When your comfort zone is riding a bike fast, being stared at by thousands of people doesn't feel right. In that last second, I just want to go. I want to get on with my job.

You feel nauseous, you want a piss or a shit or you'll suddenly want to get off the bike and lie down for a sleep. You want to be anywhere else.

There have been plenty of times when I've been all the way through that process and just about to go when suddenly, there's been a five-minute delay because a marshal hasn't been on post or the clouds have come in on the mountain. I've had 92 TT race starts and every race has made me feel the same way, whether I've been on a 250, a 400, a 600 or an electric bike. But the Superbike races are the most intense.

It's not the fact that it's a bigger bike that might be harder or faster to ride. For me, it's the kudos of getting a result on the Superbike that adds to the pressure. There have been fantastic Superstock races, and wheel-to wheel 600cc races with tenths of a second splitting the top few riders. But with the greatest of respect to all the other classes, nothing comes close to winning the blue-riband race. On the other hand, to do a 128mph on a 600 you have to hit every single mark perfectly. You have to be millimetre-accurate.

I still think that one of my best laps round the TT came on a 600. It was the final of the second Supersport race in 2013, when I finished third to Bruce Anstey and Michael Dunlop. I pipped William Dunlop by 0.4 of a second for the last spot on the podium. People might be shocked to hear me say that I think this was one of my best laps, but it was beautiful. Getting it right on a 600 is so rewarding. On the Superbike you can have a bit of a slide here and there, and recover by using power to pull you along. On the smaller bikes you need to be pinpoint accurate all the time. But they don't get the kudos they deserve because all eyes are on the big bike race.

Whatever kind of bike you're on, the first time you start going down the hill you don't know what's coming. I don't care who you are or what your name is, you do not know where your head's at. That first lap down Bray Hill is the most exciting, exhilarating, frightening and sometimes horrible experience you can ever have. You can give yourself such a fright that you fuck the whole race up within the first 30 seconds.

I don't want to give too much away but I do think a lot of what happens in a TT race stems from the start. I've seen a few big-name racers pull over on bikes that have had nothing wrong with them because they've gone down Bray Hill and their heads have gone. I've been down there holding on for grim death myself. Especially on those early Dunlop tyres we used to run, they were evil things until they had temperature and pressure in them. I've had heart-rate monitors on me for races and before I go my head is pounding and my heart is racing. I can feel it beating in my chest on the line. But as soon as I set off my heart-rate goes down. Once the adrenaline of the start has worn off and I'm doing something physical by riding the bike, I can control it again and it comes down to where it should be. When the tyres go from feeling like shit to suddenly wanting to work with you, then you can go for it.

After Crosby, it feels like the bike has settled down, maybe three or four miles in. That's when you can grab your first breather, while maintaining a winning rhythm at the same time. That's not something you can learn to do overnight, which is why I respect Peter Hickman so much. The pace that he's been able to get to within such a short space of time is amazing. It took me a long time to be able to do 125mph laps, let alone 130mph ones. Either the rest of us are shit or Peter is outstandingly brilliant.

When I'm on the bike and doing my job, I can be doing 180mph down the Sulby Straight and suddenly find myself wondering what Becky and the kids are up to. Even at that speed I can picture Maisie playing games on her iPad, Becky will be glued to the radio waiting for me to pass through each sector, and checking her phone every ten seconds. Ewan is trying to keep his cool. He's at that age now where he understands what can happen out there. When I'm on the bike his fuse gets short and he stresses a bit. Maisie is only six so it's just another day for her.

These thoughts last split seconds, then they're gone. Even at 190mph I might race through a section of the track and smell someone's BBQ cooking at the side of the road. At other times I can smell my own sweat or cow shit from the fields. I take it all in when I'm riding fast – sheep up on the mountain or the ferry pulling into the harbour. I clock the clouds moving or the helicopter tracking me. It's not that these things are distractions, I just take them in as I go. Lots of them are completely irrelevant.

Despite me obsessively needing to race the TT, the relief when I finish a race is massive. Even in a practice session, every time I cross the finishing line I think, 'I have another day on this planet. I can get some food with the kids, have a pint and live another day tomorrow.' When you come back up that return road, the feeling is amazing. I love the buzz afterwards, the chat with the team and the debrief. When I finish a Senior race it's like somebody has lifted ten bags of cement off my shoulders. The bike feels different every time round and the conditions can change every lap as well. A little moment here and a little fright there, but you have to just stay on it and go flat out all the way to the flag.

I've been lucky these last few years and have done a lot of winning. I always wonder what the guy who finished last is thinking, whether he's as proud of his finisher's medal as I am of my winner's trophy. I'm being paid to do this but that guy has put his balls and every shilling he has on the line to be there and he's getting nothing apart from a medal. I hope he feels like he's achieved his challenge like I feel I've achieved mine. When you finish sixth, it's easy to feel disappointed, but when you think about the guys at the other end of the field, it can remind you that sixth isn't so bad.

In ten years, I want to be that bloke standing on the grid with a pint in my hand. I want to look into the eyes of the guys lining up to race, knowing what they're about to embark on for the next hour and 45 minutes. I wouldn't go near them, but I'm looking forward to seeing what makes TT racers tick from the outside looking in.

CHAPTER 23

Am I a Bad Omen?

I WAS ONE of the first riders to witness Paul Shoesmith's crash in 2016. It was the worst thing I've seen, ever. It was horrendous. I'd stopped at Ballaugh Bridge to adjust my clutch and Shoey and a couple of others came by. I went back out behind them. Ballaugh to Sulby is only a couple of miles. Something went wrong at the start of the Sulby Straight. Shoey was in the middle of it and his bike was in the village at the end.

I saw David Jefferies lying in the road when he was killed and in a weird way he looked peaceful. It looked like somebody had laid him there to rest. It wasn't like that with Shoey and it'll scar me forever. I remember thinking that I can't have seen what I saw, it can't have been physically possible. Hutchy, Hillier, Johnny Barton and Stevie Heneghan had seen Shoey as well. When we got back in we were all looking at each other and I had to ask if my eyes had deceived me. My first thoughts were for his family. It fucked me up for a few days.

So a friend of mine was killed in my first TT and another one died in the most recent one I raced in. Like I say, I'm hardened to death now, but I always do the same thing when I see a crash or come across one during a road race. I pick a spot in the distance and ride for it, without moving my eyes. I don't look at it or anything around it. I just block the thing out. I'm not a medic and there's nothing I can do for anyone. That's how I deal with it. But with Shoey's crash, I had to manoeuver my bike around debris in the road and curiosity got the better of me. I wish it hadn't

No matter how long you've been riding, there is always something that can hit a nerve. When you think you've seen and done everything on track, when you think you've suffered every pain, something proves you wrong. That crash was fucking mind-blowing.

Conor's crash in 2010 was dreadful too and that crash of Stephen Thompson's at the North West in 2015 knackered me up. He bounced over the top of a garden wall coming out of York hairpin and eventually lost an arm. I didn't think he could have survived a crash like that, but he did.

I've never thought about exactly how many friends and acquaintances I've lost to road racing until now. Off the top of my head I can name 31 without even thinking about it much, and that's just since 1996. It's fucking mad. I probably am a little bit cold to death and dying. When I was growing up, my dad used to tell me if someone was killed at the TT. People I knew would talk about it and you could read about it in books and magazines about the place, so it's not like I didn't know that people die there. Long before I raced there I think I was mentally prepared for that bit. I'd already gone through it in my head and accepted that people get injured or paralysed or die at the TT. It doesn't make it any easier to take though.

Nobody dies when you're young, especially in your own family. My Nana's death was the first one I had to deal with and it was tough. I've still lost hardly any relatives and I'm 44. All my old aunties and uncles are ploughing on. My gran and grandad on my mum's side are still going strong in their mid-eighties.

Joey, DJ, Simon Andrews, Steve Hislop, Mick Lofthouse, Gus Scott, Paul Shoesmith and all the others I've mentioned who have been killed were all great guys. Looking back, I've sometimes wondered if I'd have been better off not getting to know them, considering how things ended up. I always decide that I'm glad I did. Any time that you spend with someone who becomes a friend needs to be cherished. It doesn't matter if you only get two years or ten. If you don't have that time with them, what do you have? A head full of empty memories is no good to anyone. And if you didn't want to get to know people in case something bad happened to them you'd end up going mad and never leaving the house. Have the fun, seize the moment, take the picture and create memories. It's horrible when you lose a friend. You grieve, you shed your tears but you can't dwell. I don't, anyway. I like to think of the great craic we had when things were good. But we're all different and I don't expect everyone reading this to think like I do.

I love meeting people who turn out to be characters, that's what I'll miss the most when I finish racing. I like hearing people's stories and finding out the background behind things. I also like to look into people's eyes and see what's behind them, trying to work out if they're talking shit or telling you the truth. I'm still not sure if I'm any good at working out if someone is giving me a bum steer, mind.

I do feel sorry for people who haven't lived a bit. Sometimes I'll drive to a function where everyone is going to think I'm a god and I'll be signing autographs all day. I'll pass guys in cars going the other way and wonder where they're going and what they'll be doing there. Probably looking at job sheets and trying to get to Wolverhampton by nine o'clock to sell some kitchen sinks or something, worrying that their boss is going to be all over them. I'm absolutely not knocking those people, but I'll take all the excitement and risk and fun while I can. Every one of the guys who has died has left me with some amazing memories of great times. Maybe the moral of this story is don't befriend me. I might have been a bad omen for them.

When people ask me what all this TT experience does for me, I tell them it allows me to recognise when I'm giving my best and when I need to accept that I might not have enough on the day.

The point I'm trying to make is that it's hard to know if you're going to be able to do more than you're already doing. I'm looking at Hutchy and Michael Dunlop now doing 133s, they took six seconds off my lap record. All I can think about is how? How, how, how have they done that? There aren't many days when I don't think about this and how I'm going to do it as well. I mean no disrespect to them, but it's got to be power. I have to believe that. As long as my arse points to the ground I'll believe that they didn't ride better than me. Not better on the brakes or at getting on the power, and they're not hitting better apexes than me. They can't have been. They both rode brilliantly and they beat me, they are fucking great riders.

You've got Michael Dunlop, who has so much natural ability he's pissing it out the end of his dick, and Ian Hutchinson, who has the most amazing work ethic and approach to racing, I have so much admiration for him. What you need in any sport is for it to be competitive, with guys like me, Michael and Ian, it is. It's also great to see that we're not all made from the same gravy. After that race in 2016, I sat back with a cold Corona in my hand and was happy with my performance. I couldn't have given any more.

But then I get my doubts. Am I actually that good at riding round the TT? I'm not sure. Did I come along at the right time to grab all those wins when the TT was on its arse in 2004, '05 and '06? The depth of field is so much stronger now than it was back then. Hutchy is on it, Michael has hit his stride and is unbelievably strong, Conor is always fast, and Lee Johnston and Peter Hickman could take things to the next level. It wasn't like this ten years ago. When I was having it away at the TT there was Archibald, Lougher and a few others, and I just sort of popped out at the front at the end of the races. I was on good bikes, on good tyres surrounded by good teams that looked after me as best they could. I believed in myself, especially after the help that Jim Moodie gave me in 2004. It fired me up, which helped me be quick straight out of the traps. With the greatest of respect to everybody, some of those wins felt easy. I'd go quite hard at the start of those races, put a couple of strong laps in early and then enjoy the ride all the way to the finish line.

I know that I haven't won all those TTs just because of luck and that there's something about what I do that makes me quick at that place, but I try not to think about it too much. I'd much rather just keep on enjoying my racing over there. I look at some of the guys that end up racing the TT. They float through club racing, don't really achieve much at national level and then decide to have a crack at the TT. They might be able to get around at a half-decent pace, but I'm not sure they're lining up for the right reasons. Look at Peter Hickman, he's the opposite of that. I can see the passion he has for the TT and anything else on two wheels. He's enjoying his racing and I like seeing that. It's a different approach for someone like Conor, who has grown up on the circuit and is a complete natural around the place.

*

A Superbike works in a narrow window and you have to have the confidence to push it through the level where it doesn't feel right and to the one where everything works. Then you have to keep it there for as long as you can.

A Superstock bike with treaded tyres and a bit more flex is easier to work with, which is why the racing is as close as it is in that class. Superbikes have bigger brakes, a stiffer yoke and forks, and they're harder to make work. They feel vague and stiff until you get in the right window, then you get them to do what you want them to. There aren't many people who can get a Superbike straight to that window. I feel like I'm kicking people in the cods for saying it, but I'm not. It goes back to what I was saying about the need to not overcomplicate things.

I've heard other guys saying that they have to have a MoTec, or this particular dash, or that the bike has to have data and suck them off at 12 o'clock. I've always thought that was the wrong approach. I like my bikes simple. Kit loom, kit ECU, a tuned engine but not one that wants to explode all the time. It keeps the chances of stuff going wrong to a minimum. You need to find a balance.

It's also about not letting things get in my head. I remember when Hutchy took on the factory bike that Leon Camier rode. It was full of bling, with a factory swing-arm and all that stuff, but that's not to say it was the right tool for the job. I never take my eye off what others are up to, like when TAS had full-on digital dash set ups and my bike still had a needle for a rev counter. But by keeping it simple, I've never believed that I couldn't win on the Superbike. Whether it's better than theirs or not, the combination of it and me can win.

When you get your race bike how you want it, there's a lot to be said for just taking it and doing as many laps as you can. I'd see a rival blow an engine up in practice, at which point they were learning absolutely nothing. While they were racing back to the pits to grab another bike I was just clocking up laps. People sometimes think that my bike has a magic wand on it, but it hasn't. It might not have the top speed, but my package has the right balance and consistency, and that pushes my confidence up, which makes me go faster still. It's all well and good if your team claims the top speed in practice, but where will that get them in the race? I remember TAS Suzuki claiming 206mph through the trap at Sulby one year. Where were they in the race? That top speed trap meant nothing. It was just figures on a piece of paper.

*

I'm still head over heels in love with the Isle of Man and the TT races. Everything about the place works for me, the people, the track and the history of the event. The atmosphere grabs me every time the ferry pulls into Douglas. If I was to choose anything that gets to me about it now, it would be the PR obligations. In a way, I've become a victim of my own success.

It's really hard to structure how your race fortnight is going to go at the TT. You can roll off that boat with an airtight plan, dinner at the Creg on Mad Sunday at two o'clock, then drinks on the Calf of Man that evening. It's all bullshit. You can't stick to those plans because there are always unforeseen circumstances. Bad weather, a bit of a stoppage on track, a bike breaks down and you miss some practice time. All those things can and will happen when you least want them to. But when they do, you still have to go and do that 20-minute interview that turns into a 40-minute one.

Then two more interviews on top that nobody told you about. I can just about get my head around that stuff. I know that I have to do these PR things because people want to keep up with what I'm doing. Most of the time I don't mind all, but sometimes it feels like the whole point of me being at the TT has been forgotten about. I'm a bike racer, riding at one of the most dangerous circuits on the planet. That means I need to make sure everything is as I want it, my bike, my kit and my head. That takes time and it can't be taken lightly. I'm not being ungrateful when I say the PR pressure pisses me off, I'm just doing my best to keep safe.

There's something that pisses me off even more about road racing though, and that's arguing with my missus. I hate the tension it creates. Me and Becky are pretty much inseparable, we have been since we were kids. We've had our ups and downs like any normal couple, and big arguments about whatever. But the TT does weird things to both of us. It feels like as we drive off the ferry in Douglas, someone secretly snips our fuses from five millimetres to half that, and we end up going off at each other. I don't like it at all. I don't like Becky feeling unhappy, which she does when she feels that sponsors and people in the paddock are getting more from me than I should be giving them. I don't like coming back to the campervan feeling like I've had the piss taken out of me by people wanting their pound of McGuinness flesh, when I should have been spending a bit of time with Becky and the kids. It creates tension that we don't need.

The thing is, I completely understand why she feels that way. I'd like nothing more than to shut the door on the motorhome and play Lego with Maisie until *Coronation Street* comes on, to be a dad and a husband. Instead, I end up defending why I've had to spend half an hour longer with that journalist, or do an extra lap of the course for a bus-full of sponsors when maybe I didn't have time for breakfast that day because I was doing a radio interview first thing. That side of it pisses me off because it's unnecessary time-wasting.

The time that you have before races at the TT has to be special, and for me that means spending it with Becky and the kids. I need to be able to switch off and not worry about other people and what they're trying to achieve. I think sometimes these people forget that while I can help them do their job, they can't really return the favour. If nobody knew who I was and I'd never won a TT in my life, you'd still find me in the paddock, I'd just be in a smaller motorhome, wearing leathers without as many sponsor logos and riding a bike nobody wanted to look at. I don't want to spend that time arguing and I don't want to have to stand up and shout that this could be the last night I get the chance to spend time with my family because who knows what the next race will bring.

All the shit that Becky deals with for me means that

she deserves more of my time and energy than anyone else. When I've been down she's picked me back up. Whether it was an injury, a bad race result or whatever, she's always been there for me. She's rock-like, a solid old thing. When I'm hurtling round the track at breakneck speed, she's the one freaking out about it. When I'm looking into her eyes before I drop my visor and head off, she's the one that's staring back at me and I feed off her strength. It's Becky that'll be expected to pick the pieces up if things go wrong.

I've asked myself in the past if Becky would be strong enough to raise the kids on her own should the worst happen. I think she'd do it in a heartbeat. If anything happened to me, I know that they'd all be all right. Financially she'd be okay, which means that I could rest in peace.

When I turned 40, we talked about getting married. We chatted about how if I died everything I'd leave behind would end up going to the government. My bikes, the cars, the whole lot, just because we weren't married. We'd been together for nearly our whole lives but we didn't tie the knot until a few years ago. It made sense and it still does now.

Getting married was the best thing in the world. If Becky were to turn round to me tomorrow and say she didn't love me anymore, she'd be more than welcome to half of everything that I have. Whatever I've earned racing bikes, I genuinely think she's entitled to it. I've seen other people break up and it turns into a right shit fest. She's been there right from the start and she'll be there at the end. She deserves everything I've been able to give her. I wouldn't leave a trail of shit behind me. We were attracted to each other as kids and to be honest when I see her now, I still want to get in her pants. Luckily we still have a great physical relationship. I've seen other people who have been together as long as we have who haven't been so lucky after 20-odd years. I think we remind each other of when we were young. We still act like kids with each other a lot.

She'll boss me and nip things in the bud if I'm out of line, which is fair enough because she's never wrong. Mind you, she'd never hold her hand up if she was. She'll stand there to the death and defend herself, that's what women do. She's very opinionated, particularly if someone has upset me. The worst thing I can do is tell her not to get involved; she likes to have the last say on things. The woman deserves a medal for putting up with what she's had to deal with. The easy way out would have been to marry a truck driver, get dinner on the table every day at five, then put the kids to bed at half seven so you can catch up with Emmerdale, and repeat for 40 years. That's a crap way to live though. There's no fight, no passion for life and no desire for anything. It's just a routine, more like a job than a life. Sometimes Becky can be a right bad-tempered bastard though, but I've learnt when to roll over and take one on the chin rather than wading in and having a ding dong over nothing.

I've often wondered if me and Becky arguing at the TT reminds me of listening to my mum and dad fighting when I was a kid, but I don't think it's the same kind of thing. My mum and dad were like a cat and a dog. For whatever reason, they sometimes just didn't seem to fit with each other.

Whether she's right or she's wrong, Becky has sat there for over 90 TT races for an hour and a half waiting for me to come back round. That deserves respect. She could have taken the easy option and chosen that trucker who is proud to announce he's paid the mortgage and fancies taking her out for an Indian. Together, we chose a path that went a different way. But however glamorous it might appear, it isn't an easy one to walk. I like the fact that we have had success and managed to stay grounded.

The McGuinness household is blessed with opportunities to do things that a lot of people don't have the chance to. Sometimes we end up taking it for granted a bit, but it only takes a flick through the photo albums to remind us of how far we've come and how lucky we are. One minute we're looking at a picture of me and Valentino Rossi laughing together, or a shot of the kids on holiday in America because I've been racing out there, the next it's a shot of me wearing one of Becky's jumpers in the back of a rusty race van in a freezing cold, soggy paddock in the middle of nowhere. Or Becky carrying a pile of smashed-up fairing panels back to the van because she was the only one who wanted to come and support me, and we didn't have enough money to get home, let alone buy replacement panels.

I think Becky might be over the glitz and glamour side of what I do now, but she understands that if I have commitments, then we both do. I think she might forget how blessed we are with what we can have sometimes.

She's right when she says that I'm selfish, if I wasn't married to Becky, I'd probably have 80 motorbikes in the garage rather than the 20-odd that I've got now. She keeps me on the straight and narrow. Men don't like to accept that sort of thing but we have to. It would be easy to have turned into some kind of Ronnie Rockstar, but Becky keeping our feet on the ground means I haven't changed. I might have a few more toys than I used to, but I'm still the same guy inside as when I was laying bricks and catching mussels. In fact, I'm sat here now wearing a three-day-old T-shirt and a pair of jeans that haven't been washed since I can remember. Does that sound like a rock star to you?

CHAPTER 24

The Future

I DIDN'T SEE the Guy Martin partnership coming. After racing for lots of years for lots of teams, I would have bet my last tenner on it not being Guy Martin who I was told I'd be riding with. When I got to the meeting and the penny dropped, I looked at Neil Tuxworth and thought, 'What a masterstroke from him and Honda.' The Fireblade is all new for 2017 and Guy brings a massive crowd. Apart from Valentino Rossi, he is probably the highest-profile rider in the world. Aside from all the PR that he can do for Honda and the new bike, he's led TT races before and has as much chance of winning a race as everyone else at the sharp end.

I spoke with him more in a few hours on the day we got together in Louth to announce the deal than I had in the 12 years I'd known him. He'd dropped his guard a bit now and then and slip back into silly truck-fitter mode. I just said to him that his success was up to him. I could make him faster round the TT, I know I could, but he'd need to trust me and listen to me. I like the fact that they've paired us on the same team. I was feeling a bit flat after 2016 and needed something to perk me up. The old bike was great but it was time for something new and I'm definitely getting that with the new Blade and having Guy as a teammate. He knows what he's doing round there and should go well. I've told him that he can spanner trucks forever but he can't do that with racing. He can build traction engines all day long when he's old but if he wants to win a TT, there's a narrow window of opportunity and he'll have to work for it.

In terms of what the new Fireblade might be able to do for me, I can see how it might play out. In my head, we'll get on the podium in 2017, maybe with a 133mph lap in us, but also with big talk about the changes that need to be made for it to be even better for 2018. That means a year to get it right and then a year to win on it. On the basis of my experience and the wins I've had up to now, that's how I see things working out.

I'm a massive believer in Honda and what they can achieve. If they can build a bike that's as fast as the competition in a straight line, then we can win. But it's very difficult to hit the nail on the head with a new bike and have it go straight to the top of the class at the TT. Look at the BMWs, they're the bikes to beat at the minute but that didn't happen overnight. The new Yamaha R1 took a real kick in the plums in year one as well. Making a great sports bike doesn't always equal making a great TT bike. All I can do in the meantime is ask Honda for what I want and if I don't get it, go to plan B. Problem is, I don't really do plan Bs.

The way I look at it, if a manufacturer wants to go to the Isle of Man and win TT races, they just need to pick up the results sheets and look at who is doing the winning. Hutchy, Michael Dunlop and me are employed, but we three must surely be the guys everyone wants on their bikes. I know that if I was putting the team together and I had the budget, I'd be straight on the phone to Michael and Hutchy, asking what they want to come and ride for me. I'd be my third-choice rider, then Peter Hickman, I believe he can do it. There are one or two other riders I believe in. Conor Cummins is definitely one of them.

Unfortunately, there's a business element to racing that not everyone thinks about. Sometimes things that you think are completely obvious and should definitely happen don't come together because of business. Passion and talent will only get you so far. At the sharp end of the TT, business matters as much as anything else. That said, I know that if I was on the bones of my arse and had no money to go racing, I could jump in the car and head for Batley where Padgett's are. I'd tell Clive that I was fucked and ask for help. I know for a fact that he'd give me a bike and I'd be going racing.

*

Norton offered me a boatload of money to go and ride their bike. To be honest, I wish they hadn't. It was a bit of a curveball really, and one that I didn't see coming. I thought about doing the fairy-tale thing and riding it for them, but with my hand on my heart, I want to stay with Honda and Julian, who prepares my bikes for me. Most importantly, I still believe I can win with Honda, and that's why I chose to sign another contract with them.

Of course I could have gone sniffing about for a little bit more money with someone else, but the danger with that is that the whole package might not be strong enough for me to do what I need to do. Not having the right man building and preparing my bikes means that my head wouldn't be in the right place, and if that happens, the job is cooked before I've even put my leathers on.

There are so many more elements to the perfect rider contract than the money. I didn't set out to be the richest rider in the paddock, I set out to be the fastest. The success that I've shared with Honda over the years can't be ignored and it feels like the right thing to do for me to stick with what I know. People might not believe that I'm not driven by money, that's up to them. As I've already said, maybe if I had set my stall out a bit earlier with Honda I could be earning more than I am now, but I've never paid much attention to what everyone else is earning so I don't really know where I sit on the salary scale. What I do know is that when me and Honda get things right, we win races. That's what I intend to carry on doing with them and the new Fireblade.

I think there might be a few people expecting me to put the boot into Honda a bit but I don't have the right to. First because there's not really any reason to and second, all you'd end up reading would be my side of the story, rather than hearing what they have to say about things as well. There are always two sides. Honda have pissed me off in the past and over the years Birdy was a prick at times, but so was Alistair Flanagan, who I rode for at AIM Yamaha, and I got a boatload of aggro when I went and rode in World Supersport. But that's people and that's racing. I'm sure they'd say the same of me given half the chance.

*

Retirement is a word that is in my head. It's not at the top of my list, but it's in there. I want to be able to step back and enjoy what I've earned. I want to be able to go to the ex-racers' dinners and have the chance to see my kids grow up. I deserve those things. I won't miss my heart trying to pump its way out of my ribcage before a race starts, or that sinking feeling when I don't win, or seeing friends lying dead in the road. The top and bottom of when I'll be ready to retire has nothing to do with trying to match or beat Joey's record and everything to do with me staying in one piece. Being safe matters more to me than winning races. I'm happy taking risks and pushing, but when I get the warnings, I'm prepared to roll over and accept that there'll be another time.

My dream retirement scenario would be to win the Senior, climb down off the top of the podium and take my family into the press conference to make an announcement that nobody could see coming. When I won the Senior in 2015, that's what I told myself I should have done after the race, after telling everyone how grateful I am for the amazing time I've had racing over the last 20 years. If I don't win another TT, I won't mind. If I do then great and if I matched Joey that'd be the icing on the cake, but when I set out to race the TT all those years ago, I never dreamed that I'd win as many as I have.

Finishing sixth or seventh is great, but it's not winning. I want to go out off the top step. That said, there's nothing to say I couldn't carry on riding the electric bike for another six or seven years, at the same time as being competitive at the Classic TT. Nobody is more aware than me that at the sharp end of the TT, there comes a time when you have to accept that it's time to roll over. I just hope the devil on my shoulder is man enough to tell me when that happens, rather than having the decision made for me through an injury or something else.

I've spoken to guys who have had a bit of a scare at the TT, pulled the bike up there and then and retired on the spot. I can't get my head around that. I've also heard of racers doing that after seeing something bad happen to someone else. Because it's never happened to me, I can't understand the thought process you'd have to go through to make that decision. I think that's a shitty way to go out. For me it would be a big win, taking a bow and thanking everyone for everything, and that would be that.

It'll be nice when I'm finished racing to be able to give something back. The sport of road racing, the people who work within the industry and the fans have given me so much pleasure. I wouldn't mind doing some hospitality work. I've been looking into the possibility of turning an old double-decker bus into a TT fan wagon. That'd be something for me to get my teeth into that I'd enjoy, while giving something back to the tens of thousands who have supported me over my career. I want people to be able to enjoy learning what the TT and its history is all about, and to help fans get an idea of what it means to those of us who know what it's like to stand on the top step having won one. It'd be a chance to share the ups and the downs that the TT gives you. That emotional rollercoaster is a ride worth experiencing and if you can't compete, what better way to get a feel for it than through someone who has not only experienced it all, but is happy to give his time and energy back to the sport? Who knows, maybe it's something that my kids could work with me on.

Either way, when I do finish racing, it'll be nice to wake up and not have to worry about the constant pressure of performing, or to get to the end of the day and be able to enjoy a beer without thinking about what it's doing to my body. It'll be nice just to live.

One thing I do worry about when it comes to retiring from the sharp end is that I've seen other riders get a bit bitter about the whole thing when they stop. There's nothing worse than hearing someone say that they could have done so much more if they'd had this bike or that bike, or if they'd had the opportunities that others might have had. To me it sounds like they're in denial a bit. But I won't know how that feels until I get there. I just hope I'm able to look back and smile at what I've achieved, rather than moaning about what I didn't.

It'd be crazy if I wasn't thinking about what retirement might look like for me. It's coming and it makes sense for me to have a plan for how I'll spend my time when I don't have to think about riding flat-out for money. I'd like to be able to do something fairly easy. With the greatest of respect, I feel like I've earned the right to. I've always had a bit of a plan for most things and when I look into my crystal ball, I see my future being one in which I'm still surrounded by bikes.

We've just moved into a house on the outskirts of Morecambe. The place we've bought has loads of land. I like the idea of hosting an event once or twice a year for bikers. There's 15 acres, which is more than enough room to camp on, park hundreds of bikes, put a band on and make a bit of noise without annoying the neighbours. There aren't really any neighbours to annoy.

I know I'll always ride bikes, whether it's up to the shops on my Africa Twin or having a wobble round in an enduro event near my house. My dad still rides bikes so why shouldn't I? He's got a 1200 Bandit and is a bit of a cannon on it to be fair. I'm expecting to take the phone call one day that he's in a big heap somewhere because he's stuffed the thing into a bush or something. He's had a few moments but he won't be told, so I don't bother trying any more. I can't do anything more than cross my fingers and hope that he doesn't kill himself on the thing. If he does, I'd have to say that maybe it was meant to be. We've spent our entire lives surrounded by motorbikes, so it wouldn't come as a surprise to me if they were with us to the very end.

When it comes to riding on the roads for fun, I've calmed down a lot as I've got older. I think I'd choose my Africa Twin over my Fireblade for a road ride nowadays. That should tell you everything you need to know about how I think when I'm not racing.

Things still get a bit spiky when I'm off-roading though. Two of my best friends that I kick around with are 53 years old. One of them is a guy called Mick, we've been friends for years. He's never raced a bike in his life, but when we're off-road I can't keep up with him. He's spent his whole life spraying bumpers, no thoughts and dreams about racing, but he's just got feel for what a bike is doing under him. I want to be like that when I'm his age, to enjoy my riding and still be quick, without putting myself under any pressure to compete.

The other guy is called Peter Carr, he's an ex-international Speedway rider and the racing fire still burns in his belly. When the three of us are out, you can see he still wants to have it. I like dirt-bike riding and when I retire, I hope I can find more time to enjoy it.

Our kid is better than me on a MX bike now as well. I regularly ride off-road with Kurt. He went through the same competitive process with my dad as me, but with Go Karts rather than motorbikes. When I moved onto working with professional teams, my dad was no longer really involved and he was chomping at the bit to get involved with some kid of racing. Kurt got to the age where they could go racing together so they did. I used to watch my dad cheating like mad, filing the exhaust ports down with a hand file and doing whatever he could to make Kurt's Kart go quicker. I've also seen him throwing cylinders across the room when he's been kicked out of a race for breaking the rules.

I went with them to Three Sisters racetrack in Wigan to watch Kurt once. He was leading the race in the wet, then the track dried out and he dropped back down the field. My dad was in a right old rage. He was stood on the banking punching himself in the head, proper angry dad stuff.

Kurt was pretty quick in a Kart and like I said, he smokes me on an MX bike now. He always thinks he has a lot to live up to on a bike because of what I've achieved and it upsets me a bit really. When he tells me he has big shoes to fill I just say 'have you bollocks'. We've come out of the same dick, but we're different people driven by different things. I don't like the idea of him putting himself under pressure just because he's a McGuinness. Motorbikes need to be enjoyed. If you aren't doing that, there's no point getting on them in the first place.

Every single word from the heart and completely honest, it's the best way to be. I'm still not sure how I can have lost as many close friends as I have and still feel the need to line up to race at the TT every year. All I know is that as long as I'm still sharp enough to run where I want to be, the lawn will get mowed, the van will be packed full of bikes and I'll be queuing up for the boat to Douglas with everyone else. I know road racing looks completely selfish to some of you and I don't expect everyone who has read this book to understand why we feel the need to do what we do. But imagine for a second how dull life would be if we all thought the same and if we were all scared of the same spiders. I still get that explosive injection in my brain I mentioned when I saw road racing for the first time filling me with the same rush every time I fly down Bray Hill, even after all these years. It's not the winning that keeps me coming back, it's not the idea of matching or even beating Joey's record and it's certainly not the money. Riding as fast as you can on a motorbike, around the most exciting and dangerous road riding circuit on the planet is a hard thing to stop doing. Especially when you're built for the job.

Thanks

2016 FELT LIKE the right time to put a book together. I'm still a competitive rider, which means the story is far from over, but at the same time, I've got plenty to tell and wanted to get it down on paper before I got too old and too knackered to remember half of it. Also, the TT is riding high at the moment. Six or seven years ago the place felt empty, now it is heaving every year. More and more people are making the effort to come over and support us while we do what we do. Spectating at the TT has turned into a bit of a bucket-list job and I like that.

There are almost too many people to thank for their help over the course of my career, but I'd like to start by thanking my family. My amazing wife, Becky, and our two kids, Ewan and Maisie. Becky has put up with a lot and has gifted us two beautiful children. I'd also like to thank my mum and dad, as without their help I have no doubt at all that you'd be reading a book about bricklaying and not a lot else. Also, Becky's mum and dad, who took me in and treated me like a son of their own, and finally, my Nana – a lady that raised me, fed me and became my biggest supporter. I hope I've made her and the rest of my family proud.

I could write an entire book full of the names of people who I'd like to thank for their time, effort and input over the course of my career. Here is a list of as many as I can remember. Those who know me and haven't made the list will know not to take it personally. They'll probably be amazed that I've managed to remember as much as I have to get this many words down on paper.

1. Billy Ingram
Made me understand carburation gearing etc on my KR1S.

2. Uncle Dave
Buying me my first van which broke down a lot but he always came out to recover us.

3. Phil Rogerson
Local plumber, lent me a few quid to get going in 2004 and put a shower in my Iveco.

4. David Payne
Had a local bike shop that helped me out a bit with some parts and still helps to this day.

5. Nigel Bosworth / Steve Sawford
They were the top 250 jockeys and gave some of there old parts for my TZ.

6. Phil Plater from Dunlop
Top bloke, used to save me all the best part worn tyres out of the Dunlop skip.

7. My dad's mate Alister
Bought a few bits for my Kawasaki in the early days.

8. Frank Wrathall
Man that made my bike fast and reliable, super respect for him.

9. Ricky Leddy
Just one of the unsung heros of the job, owe this guy for two TT wins.

10. The Morris brothers
Neil and Lee (lynal viynal) won the last ever singles TT on their special bike.

11. Glyn Ormerod
One of my best mates that I smuggled over to the Isle of Man to help mechanic at my first TT.

12. Ian Whitlow

We had so much success at the TT with him by my side, we were best mates, but he crashed a bike I lent him at the North West in 2009 and he's never spoken to me since?!

13. Charlotte Pullan (Lee Pullan's wife)

For just having the same date of birth as me and being my number 1 fan.

14. Lynne Pete and family from Selby

They brought the 'chuck van' to the races to feed the troops.

15. The Jefferies family

Dave's mum would look after Ewan while Becky would watch me.

16. Pit board crew at the TT

The information is so important, big Ian Mac at Ballacraine, Ben for years at Gwens who passed away a few years ago and Nat at the Bungalow who stands for hours in shit weather!

17. The boys that took over from Ben

Mick, Dave, Dacka, old father etc etc!!! These pricks write all sorts of shite on the board.

18. Andy Smith from Yamaha

Congratulates me now even when I win on a Honda.

19. Phil Wain

Great bloke that's done my press releases for years.

20. Mick Rayner

Best man at my wedding, educated me with some business decisions, sometimes feel like I take the piss out of him, he, to be fair, sorts everything out for me! Because I'm useless. Couldn't cope without him.

21. Karen and Chris Merkel

They do all my invoicing for me, she keeps me on my toes, Chris is the best sticker man.

22. Mike Hayton

Saved my career by repairing my knackered wrist.

23. John the train driver

Looks after me on my train journeys.

24. Karen and Dave

We couldn't cope without these guys at the TT for over 13 years, even though they turn the paddock into a gypsy village.

25. John & Kath Jones
Loyal sponsors and family friends.

26. Sam Neate
Our adopted son! Do anything for us, always has a trendy comb-over though.

27. Ste Bartlett
Family friend, do anything for us, ginger though and they are nearly extinct.

28. Mark Davis
Big boss at Honda when I went back to Honda in 2006, proper fair guy, had and still got lots of respect for him.

29. Dave Hancock
Another Honda boss, was all for the racers and the best-dressed man on the planet.

30. Jonathon Martin
Sponsor that took things to the next level and become a family friend.